Morecock, Fartwell, & Hoare

MORECOCK
FARTWELL
&
HOARE

A Collection of
Unfortunate but True Names

Russell Ash

St. Martin's Press ⚏ New York

www.stmartins.com

Library of Congress Cataloging-in-Publication Data

Ash, Russell.
    [Potty, Fartwell & Knob]
    Morecock, Fartwell, & Hoare : a collection of
unfortunate but true names / Russell Ash. — 1st
U.S. ed.
        p. cm.
    Originally published: Potty, Fartwell & Knob.
London : Headline. 2007.
    ISBN 978-0-312-54535-2
    1. Names, personal—Great Britain—Humor.
2. Names, personal—Humor. I. Title. II. Title:
Morecock, Hoare and Fartwell.
PN6231.N24A84 2009
929.40941—dc22

                                        2009024038

Originally published as Potty, Fartwell & Knob in Great
Britain by Headline Publishing Group

First U.S. Edition: November 2009

10 9 8 7 6 5 4 3 2 1

To anyone who has ever had a strange name

Contents

Nutty Haddock

Introduction

Fiction and fact

When I told my family and friends I was compiling a book of strange but true British names, almost all of them responded with, 'I was at school with someone called…' Some – though, sadly, not all – of the names they suggested turned out to be true, but I soon discovered that those that were true represented only the tip of the onomastic* iceberg. Beneath the surface, hidden away in parish registers, birth, marriage and death records and official censuses, lie countless millions of undiscovered names spanning nine hundred years (the earliest here dates from 1109), from which I have excavated the few thousand that appear in this book.

And what names! Britain, the country that gave us toilets made by Thomas Crapper and a James Bond actor called Roger Moore, has a long tradition of odd and *double entendre* names that feature in our literature and comedy. The names invented, or adapted, by Charles Dickens represent just one stop on a comedic branch line that in the twentieth century gave us the Starkadders of *Cold Comfort Farm*; *The Goons* (Grytpype-Thynne and Willium Cobblers); the *Carry On* films (W. C. Boggs, Sidney Ruff-Diamond, *et al*); *Round the Horne* (J. Peasmold Gruntfuttock, Sid Rumpole, Dame Celia

*Relating to names

Molestrangler); *Monty Python* (Gervais Brookhamster, Raymond Luxury-Yacht – pronounced Throatwobbler Mangrove), Rowan Atkinson's school register sketch from *The Secret Policeman's Ball* (which includes several – Dint, Nibble, Mattock and Soda – that actually exist), and so on. However, even Dickens' most fanciful Sweedlepipes, Honeythunders and Fezziwigs do not come close to the reality of the aberrant but genuine first names, surnames and name combinations you are about to encounter.

Such factors as our tradition of eccentricity, linguistic changes, attempts by parents to come up with an original name and the blunders of illiterate scribes have combined to create the massive names catalogue of Britain, and this is the first ever attempt to present a selection of the strangest examples from this remarkable collection.

SEYMOUR PUSSY

'There's one born every minute'

This has not been true in the UK for over a century: today, more than 1.2 babies are born every minute in England and Wales alone, and every one of them has to be named.

Some are born with strange surnames, some are blessed, or cursed, with unusual first or middle names. Occasionally we encounter such 'joke' names as Ben Dover (though there have been several real ones), or news reports of peculiar but inadvertent names, like the couple who as recently as 2004 innocently named their son 'Drew Peacock', before people started to say, 'You called him *what*…?'

Aside from a few whimsical names, some bowing to the inevitable (if your surname is Christmas, you may as well call your kid 'Merry' – everyone else will), and some ludicrously long names, which are frankly irresistible, the majority were 'accidental', not deliberately designed to attract attention or raise a laugh. The ever-crazier names inflicted on the offspring of celebrities and the bizarre excesses of deed poll name changes have been avoided. I have also resisted delving into the realm of 'nominative determinism', the tendency for people to end up in professions appropriate to their names, as in the style of the famous I. Pullem, dentist, although I have included the occasional serendipitous discovery, such as Abraham Ball, castrator, such ironies as the birth of George Fatman in Broadbottom, Cheshire, and the weddings of Holmes and Watson, Bell and Bottoms and Fucks and Allott and their ilk.

Where did these names come from?

Many surnames were originally descriptive – including those that refer to an individual's character or physical defects or are otherwise insulting – but the embarrassment associated with such names or those containing a *double entendre* depends on literacy and communications, which, before the modern era, were both undeveloped. Until recent times, most people were born, married and died within a few miles of their home. They probably could not read or write, so never sent or received letters, did not have any forms to fill out or phone calls to answer, did not travel abroad and hence did not need passports, so if someone happened to be called William Bollocks, it was perfectly possible for him to keep it quiet from the world beyond his family circle and so avoid being the subject of derision.

Page Turner

Some of the oddities result from the incongruity of the first and second names or the perhaps unwitting choice of a first name that, when written as an initial, teams aptly or inaptly with the surname – hence I. Pod and C. Rap.

Some bearers of strange names were perhaps immigrants whose names were unremarkable in their own countries, such as Low Fat, who married in Cardiff in 1905. However, other than such individuals, or a few immigrants who fetch up in British censuses, all the names are of British people.

PLEASANT TITTY

Source material

After pornography, genealogy has become one of the most popular uses of the Internet, and it is only through access to online material that I have been able to research and compile this book – previously it would have been well-nigh impossible.

To unearth these names I have mined parish registers for records of baptisms, marriages and burials, wills and other legal documents, newspapers and phone books. The registration of births, marriages and deaths in England and Wales has been compulsory only since 1837. National censuses have been held every ten years since 1841 (though we currently have free access only to those up to 1901).

These sources present information of variable detail: in the case of some baptisms, we may know the names of one or both parents; with marriages, sometimes the name of the spouse; and with deaths and burials we often know the age. Census returns identify professions, but give ages rather than dates of birth, so birth years are *circa*, rather than precise.

Eureka!*

The frisson of discovering these names has been a constant pleasure. Surely no one can ever have been called Fanny Plenty – it's just too similar to *Goldfinger*'s Pussy Galore or *Austin Powers'* homage, Alotta Fagina – but, amazingly, there are several. Dick Head? Of course. Penis Hardon? Naturally. It

*Eureka Jones, born Kingswinford, Staffordshire, c.1876

is therefore almost disappointing to find that there is, for example, a Mary Dupp but not a May Dupp, a John Time but not a Justin Time, and a Thomas Handcart but not a Helena Handcart. If only their parents had had more imagination.

Surely, some mistake?

Some peculiar names may have resulted from an error or mis-transcription. In 1857 the Registrar-General reported that of 159,097 couples signing the marriage registers in England and Wales, 115,085 men wrote their names, and 44,013 (28 per cent of the total) made their marks. Among women, 97,332 signed and 61,765 (38 per cent) made their marks, the total rising to more than half in some counties. When so many of the adult population of the country could not even write their own names, it is no surprise that the registers contain some bizarre spellings, phonetic versions or inspired guesses.

The census returns to which we have access are copies, not the originals, which were destroyed long ago, in handwriting that ranges from elegant copperplate script to spidery scrawl, and contain many obvious errors. These have often been com-pounded when transcribed yet again into electronic databases. One of my own ancestors, whose

Ivor Hardon

not especially unusual first name was 'Drusilla', appears in the 1861 census as 'Priscilla' and in 1871 as 'Omsilla', while her daughter, also called Drusilla, appears as 'Prusella' in 1861 and 'Orusilla' in the 1871 census. Thus Pubica Prestridge (1841 census) turns out to be Isabella Partridge and Joseph Prickhead (1901 census) is disappointingly Joseph Pritchard. To avoid such traps, wherever possible original documents have been checked and, as a result, what might have been some splendidly dippy names, eliminated. A few may have slipped through the net and I will be delighted to receive any corrections.

Census spoofs

There is evidence of occasional spoof entries in census returns. They were in all probability created by bored transcribers, the best-documented of which is the imaginative cast of characters inhabiting a Chelsea lodging house in 1881. It included Charles Bigtop – tiger slayer; Gustave Stinkpoor – turpentine boiler; Tanta Toppie – boy hairdresser; Henry Dandelion – horsehair plaiter; William Pitt – clown; and 90-year-old Jimy [*sic*] Hillad – peacock carrier. Not far away, at the fictitious Paddington address of '16 Acacia Gardens', we find a 52-year-old 'international playboy', his 97-year-old wife and son (occupation –'ponce') and a cosmopolitan army of servants, among them a Timbuktu-born butler, a Persian governess, a Russian gardener and a footman from Afghanistan.

Naming fashions

Naming fashions come and go over time. Though an unscientific sampling, certain years seem to have been especially strong for silly multiple names: 1842 and 1843, for example, produced Elizabeth Wrench Wrench, Mary Ann Morecock Morecock, Hairby Rook Rook, Harriot Whore Whore, Raper Raper and Edmund Crisp Crick Crick.

Certain locations are also notable for the oddity of their inhabitants' names: St George Hanover Square, London registered such names as Charles Penis Horn and Emma Dyke Dyke. I can also corroborate the observations of researchers since the Victorian period who noted that Bury St Edmunds, Suffolk and Guildford, Surrey have a disproportionate abundance of strange names. I would also nominate Sculcoates, Yorkshire; Mitford, Norfolk; Portsea Island, Hampshire; and Blything, Suffolk.

Some names were not considered odd when they were created, but language marches on and linguistic changes mean that certain people find themselves lumbered with weird or *double entendre* names. As a result of such changes and increasing awareness, certain names have fallen out of favour or bizarre names altered and so filtered out of Britain's names corpus – which may explain, for example, why there is hardly anyone with the surname Titty after about 1830, and why the once hugely popular Fanny (as a given name, rather than a nickname for girls born 'Frances') all but vanished by the First World War.

The uniqueness of some first names can be fairly simply explained as an aberration that never caught on. Only half a dozen people seem to have received 'Spearmint' as a first or middle name – all but one of them in 1906 – while only one person appears ever to have been baptized 'Bovril' (Bovril Simpson, who married in West Ham, 1911).

GLADYS FRIDAY

So good they named them twice

Some names are the human equivalents of the tautonyms encountered in the world of zoology, where the genus and species names are identical, as with *Alces alces* (the moose), *Cygnus cygnus* (the whooper swan), *Ratus ratus* and *Gorilla gorilla* (you'll never guess). Can it just be down to pride in one's family name that leads so many parents to repeat it as their child's middle name – hence those previously noted, along with Mabel Sexey Sexey, Henry Basher Basher, Bold Bold, James Brook Dust Dust, Lucinda Legassick Legassick and Albert Fluck Fluck?

Cruelty to children

It is impossible to fathom the psychology behind many naming decisions. Take, for example, those who had a weird name

– Rhoda Boat, Henry Fuckalls, Henrietta Prick, Epaphreditus Eatty, Eva Brick, Prudentia Doolittle, Seraphim Hooker, Humiliation Hinde, Hercules Anthill, Golden Balls, Kitty Moose, Noble Wasp, Dansey Dansey, Large Bee and Grimwood Death, to name but a few – and promptly give their own offspring the same name. Were their parents proud of the names and desperate to see them carried on to the next generation, or is there perhaps a sense of, 'I had to put up with it – now you can too'?

Names occasionally serve as a parental commentary on the latest and perhaps unwelcome addition to the family, hence Lewis Unexpected Smith, Not Wanted James Colvill, No More Durrant, One Too Many Gouldstone, Finale Eldridge, Franklin Addenda Wilkins and (allegedly) That's It Who'd Have Thought It Restell.

NORMAN CONQUEST

The servant problem
Census returns in particular reveal that many of the bearers of 'embarrassing' names are servants. This is partly explained by their sheer numbers: at the time of the 1901 census there were 1,285,072 female servants out of a total female population of 16,804,347 in England and Wales – in other words, one woman in every thirteen was in service. There is also more than a hint of discrimination: masters and mistresses would often dub their staff with jokey or easily recalled variants of their real names, or nicknames that duly found their way into census returns.

Where have all the funny names gone?
Anyone undertaking genealogical research cannot fail to be moved by the constant reminders of high infant mortality

before the twentieth century. All too often a birth or baptism is rapidly followed by a record of his or her death, so there was no chance of their passing their surname on by marriage, or, as noted above, by handing it on to their children as an often unwelcome gift.

Unusual surnames borne by women were lost when they were changed through marriage. In the 1841 census, there were fifteen people bearing the unfortunate surname 'Myass'. One of the last recorded, Ann Myass, married in 1886, thereby changing her name. By the time of the 1901 census, there were none. Or consider John Scum: we know he married in 1838, but there is no record of any Scum kids: did he and Mrs Scum not have any little Scums, or did they perhaps change their surname to something less pejorative?

Name changes are by no means a modern phenomenon: Joshua Bug's decision to change his name to Norfolk Howard was announced in *The Times* on 26 June 1862. Or John Robert Shittler, born in 1851 in Wimborne, Dorset, who married Martha Reeve in Kingston, Surrey, in 1877. Love conquers almost everything, but maybe not quite enough to spend the rest of your life as a Shittler, and so, in 1884, Mr Shittler changed his family name to Rowden.

A sort of natural selection may have eliminated some surnames: most women would prefer not to marry if it meant thereby acquiring an embarrassing surname, so the name was not perpetuated, though some were not too lucky in their choices. Take, for instance, Ada Nudy: bad enough to have such a name, but in 1913 she married Harry Bott, thereby becoming the even less desirable Mrs Harry Bott. Other women traded a ghastly surname for a worse one, as did Mary Madcap when in 1782 she married John Bastard. Some forethought might have saved a girl who was allegedly but charmingly named Wild Rose from the unfortunate combination that resulted from her marriage to a Mr Bull. And pause for a moment to consider the devotion of Ann Smith, who loved William Fuck enough to marry him.

Past and present

Morecock, Fartwell, & Hoare takes us on a tour of the major cities and tiny hamlets of a Britain peopled by so many oddly named characters that in some respects it appears another country or the setting of some surreal sitcom. Yet, while names of the past inevitably form the bulk of those that follow, the story has not ended: names such as Radar Oo, Princess Diana Frempong, Su Doku, Phoenix Claw Unicorn, Jago Pirate Turner and Icicle Star Crumplin all date from the twenty-first century.

Finally, don't forget, I had only to disinter these names, and you have only to read – and, I hope – enjoy them. These people spent their lives with them!

Notes

• The humour derived from some names depends on the not unreasonable expectation that their owners' short forms were used on occasion – Richard was commonly known as 'Dick', Philip as 'Phil', and so on.

• Some rely on their pronunciation – the seemingly innocuous 'Mike Hunt', for example, sounds like – well, you get the idea. If you don't get them, try saying them out loud (though perhaps not too loud, and not in a public place).

• Gender is noted where it is not obvious from the name or context, but the sex of some is impossible to interpolate from the available data.

• Apologies for the prevalence of Fannies but it was once one of the most common female names – and it is very funny.

• Especially when infant mortality was high, baptisms usually followed soon after births. Baptisms were entered in the parish register, so we know the date and location, and often the names of both parents; we generally don't know, but can reasonably assume that the place of birth was in the same locality.

• Place of birth is noted where known, but it is either omitted or given at county level only in some sources, such as early censuses; 'np' means no place and 'nd' no date is indicated in the source.

• The location of a registered birth is often the registration district – usually the nearest town with a register office – but not necessarily the exact place of birth, although these are recorded in census returns with either greater (down to parish level) or lesser ('London' or 'Dorset', for example) precision.

• 'Census' is for England unless otherwise stated.

• Locations and county names are as they were at the time of the record – in some instances, places may now be in different counties: for example, Barnet moved from Hertfordshire (1837–51) to Middlesex (1852–1946) and back to Hertfordshire (1946–65) before becoming part of Greater London (1965–present); Wokingham was in Wiltshire until 1845, but is now in Berkshire. Readers may be surprised to see occasional Irish entries, but from 1801 to 1922 Ireland was part of the United Kingdom.

ERASMUS BUGGER

Warning
The Author and Publishers can accept no responsibility if you use this book to choose your baby's name.

Russell Ash
Lewes, 2009

Chapter One

THE GOOD THE BAD AND THE UGLY

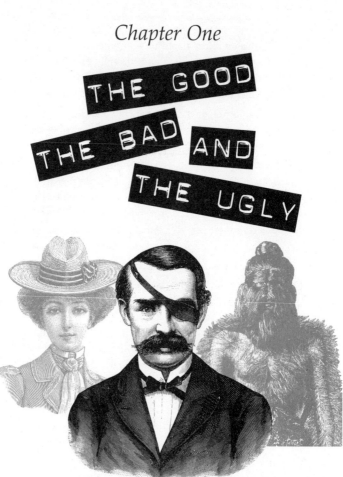

*In which we meet a diverse array of people
whose names are remarkable, baffling, uncategorizable,
or just plain weird.*

—A—

Alf Abbet
Born Teddington, Middlesex, c.1849 (Teddington, 1891 census)

George Sneezum Acock
Born Woolwich, London, 1873

Herbert Slap Aldhous
Born Islington, London, 1874

Agent Mildred Allsop
Born Barrow upon Soar, Leicestershire, 1904

Phil Ander
Born Westminster, London, c.1842
(St Martin-in-the-Fields, London, 1871 census)

Furious Andrews
(Female) Born Great Horwood, Buckinghamshire, c.1821
(Steeple Claydon, Buckinghamshire, 1881 census)

B. Ann Angel
(Female) Born Bedwelty, Monmouthshire, 1894

Onesiphorous Ankers
Married Blackburn, Lancashire, 1910

John Anonymous
Born np c.1865; died West Ham, Essex, 1868

Rameses Arblaster
Born Cannock, Staffordshire, 1910

Ann Archy
Born Haslingden, Lancashire, 1886

Annie Argument
Born Durham 1887

Wow Ashworth
(Female) Born Lancashire c.1771 (Blackburn, Lancashire, 1841 census)

Herbert Abcdef Atkinson
Born Tynemouth, Northumberland, 1904

Betty Auckward
Baptized All Saints, Hereford, 6 June 1755

—B—

Fairest Babbett
Died Manchester, Lancashire, 1864

Eileen Back
Born Merthyr Tydfil, Glamorgan, 1908

Helen Back
Born Tiverton, Devon, 1849

Shepherdess Jane Backhoffner
Born St Marylebone, London, 1845 (St Marylebone, 1851 census)
Shepherdess was the daughter of George H. Backhoffner, Professor of Chemistry and Natural Philosophy and Registrar of Births & Deaths.

Ptolemy Tom Backholer
Born Sherborne, Dorset, 1872

Bedding Badding
Born Holborn, London, c.1889 (Lambeth, London, 1901 census)

Lilian Comforter Badman
Born West Ham, Essex, 1902

Earthly Emma Bailey
Born Mitford, Norfolk, 1879

Bertram Cannon Ball
Born Stourbridge, Worcestershire, 1875

Intercydonia M. Ball
(Female) Married James Jarvis, Wolstanton, Staffordshire, 1912

Mother Balmforth
Born Bramley, Yorkshire, 1866

Banger Balster
Married Manchester, Lancashire, 1855

Aberycusgentylis Balthropp
Baptized Iver, Buckinghamshire, 25 January 1648

Dimple H. Bangle
(Male) Born Barnstable, Devon, c.1825 (Instow, Devon, 1871 census)

Piggy Banks
Born Kimmeridge, Dorset, c.1810 (East Stonehouse, Devon, 1851 census)

Fud Barbee
Born Scotland *c.*1853 (on ship *Bride of the Nile*, Humber, 1871 census)

Ali Barber
Baptized Inveresk with Musselburgh, Midlothian, 29 August 1731

William Y. Barfly
Born Penmaenmar, Caernarvonshire, *c.*1864
(Leck, Lancashire, 1881 census)

Joseph XXX Barkass
Married Newcastle upon Tyne, Northumberland, 1855

Zerrubabel Barraclough
Born Keighley, Yorkshire, 1879

Faith Hope And Charity Barratt [one person]
Born Exeter, Devon, 1846

Lilian Fluffy Barrett
Born Shoreditch, London, 1895

Thomas Honeybun Bartlett
Born Weymouth, Dorset, 1877

Monte Cristo T. Barton
Born Lambeth, London, 1898

Boadicea Basher
Baptized St Hilary, Cornwall, 13 January 1856

William Bashful
Born Staffordshire *c.*1847 (Spitalfields, London, 1871 census)

Bertie Basin
Born Holborn, London, *c.*1891 (Clerkenwell, London, 1901 census)

Fancy Baskett
Married Steyning, Sussex, 1880

Sosthenes Bather
Died Colchester, Essex, 1847

Thomas Grain Thought Bays
Married City of London, 1841

New Year Beadle
(Female) Married James Theaker, Thorne, Lincolnshire, 1862

Mercy Beak
Married Bath, Somerset, 1870

Hula Beanland
Born Burnley, Lancashire, 1871

Choo Ah Beano
Married Stepney, London, 1882

Astynax Beattle
Born Burghfield, Berkshire, c.1855 (Dorking, Surrey, 1871 census)

Harry Beatup
Born Eastbourne, Sussex, c.1878 (Eastbourne, 1881 census)

John Sidney Six Beckham
Born Norwich, Norfolk, 1860

Eleazer Bed
Born Whitechapel, London, 1871

Gaylord Beebe
Born Ashton-under-Lyne, Lancashire, 1892

Sarah Pudentia Beeks
Married Bala, Merionethshire, 1868

Bess Befor
Baptized St Giles without Cripplegate, London, 26 July 1629

Bozy Bench
Born Calverton, Nottinghamshire, c.1889 (Calverton, 1891 census)

May Snow Bennett
Born Plymouth, Devon, 1893

Thomas Churchreform Bennett
Married Faversham, Kent, 1858

Rob Bery
Born Whitechapel, London, 1857

Tunu Bibi
Born np 1938; died St Albans, Hertfordshire, 1998
*Tunu is said to be a Miwok Indian name meaning
'deer thinking about going to eat wild onions'.*

Annice Bible
Born Wolstanton, Staffordshire, 1907

Uretha Jane Biddle
Born Nottingham 1889

Betty Big
Baptized Rolvenden, Kent, 17 January 1762

Smallhope Biggs
(Male) Born Cranbrook, Kent, c.1556

Old Bill
Died Newcastle upon Tyne, Northumberland, 1906

Spanner Bing
Born Northwood, Isle of Wight, c.1822
(Newchurch, Hampshire, 1851 census)

Eliza Dribble Bingham
Married Chesterfield, Derbyshire, 1862

Beasley Bingo
(Male) Married Elizabeth Davies, Orleton, Herefordshire, 29 May 1681

Annie Primate Binnington
Married Sculcoates, Yorkshire, 1880

John Wheeler Binns
Born Wellington, Shropshire, 1874

Al Bino
Born St Marylebone, London, c.1860 (Southwark, London, 1871 census)

Parky Bishop
Died Pontypridd, Glamorgan, 1880

Simon Straight Bishop
Born np c.1818; died St Columb, Cornwall, 1871

Matt Black
Born Felling, Durham, c.1861 (Holmside, Durham, 1891 census)

Thomas John Dosias Four Blackwell
Born Morpeth, Durham, 1842

Minnie Moon Blagg
Born Basford, Nottinghamshire, 1880

Trueheart Blanchard
Died Spilsby, Lincolnshire, 1839

Marmaluke Bland
Married Spilsby, Lincolnshire, 1888

Silence Bliss
(Female) Born Woodend, Northamptonshire, c.1846
(Blakesley, Northamptonshire, 1871 census)

Strain Blogg
Born Norfolk c.1773 (South Erpingham, Norfolk, 1841 census)

Emma Bloodisack
Born Rotherhithe, London, c.1858 (Hackney, 1881 census)

Phalliss Bloomer
Born Cradley, Worcestershire, c.1876 (Litchurch, Derbyshire, 1881 census)

Mary L. Blotto
Born Lambeth, London, 1911

Bill Board
Born Abergavenny, Monmouthshire, c.1890 (Abergavenny, 1891 census)

Water Board
Born Axbridge, Somerset, 1853

Kiss Bobby
(Female) Born Diss, Norfolk, c.1853 (Fersfield, Norfolk, 1871 census)

Liar Bodwell
(Male) Born Manchester, Lancashire, c.1884
(Ince-in-Makerfield, Lancashire, 1901 census)

Annie Body
Born Plympton St Mary, Devon, 1866

Bold Bold
Married Salford, Lancashire, 1838

Nora Bone
Born South Stoneham, Hampshire, 1902

Fuku Nozwara Boogert
Born np 1935; died Hammersmith, London, 1988

Risque Booth
Born Stockport, Cheshire, 1909

Julius Caesar K. Borgia
Born St Andrews, Middlesex (Holborn, London, 1871 census)

Friend Bottle
Born Middlesex c.1816 (St Botolph, Aldersgate, London, 1841 census)

Pop Botts
(Male) Born Dorset c.1878 (Bournemouth, Hampshire, 1891 census)

Bridget Bouncer
Baptized Dunchideock, Devon, 23 October 1659

Sarah Bouncy
Married Bishop's Stortford, Hertfordshire, 1876

Honour Bound
Buried St Pinnock, Cornwall, 1783

Spartacus Martial Bourdin
Born Hendon, Middlesex, 1890

Faintnot Isaday Bourne
Born Rye, Sussex, 1878

Geronimo Bow
(Male) Married Cathe [sic] Williams, St George in the East, London, 1810

Charles Damp Bowden
Born Portsea Island, Hampshire, 1895

Affability Box
Baptized St John Horsleydown, Bermondsey, London, 3 March 1822

Ima Box
Born Reading, Berkshire, c.1865 (Reading, 1871 census)

Wallop Brabazon
Married Jane Du Pre, St Marylebone, London, 19 March 1796

Herbert Superbus Bradbury
Born Chorlton, Lancashire, 1908
His middle name is assumed to be 'Superb-us', as in Roman prefect
Marcus Superbus, rather than 'Super-bus'.

Amelia Disturnal Brassington
Born West Bromwich, Staffordshire, 1871

Susan Brasso
Baptized Wisborough Green, Sussex, 12 December 1602

Lettice Bray
Baptized Mobberley, Cheshire, 26 April 1807

Richard Clencher Brazier
Born Wolverhampton, Staffordshire, 1840

Freezer Breeze
Born Great Yarmouth, Norfolk, c.1839 (Great Yarmouth, 1851 census)

Eva Brick
(Female) Born Turkey c.1874 (Battersea, London, 1901 census)

Napoleon Lavoisier Voltaire Briggs
Married West Bromwich, Staffordshire, 1862

Jucy [*sic*] Ann Brocklebank
Born Bootle, Cumberland, 1871

Foetus Brocklehurst
Born Prestwich, Lancashire, 1877

Napkin Brooker
Married Mary Hawkins, St Michael, Lewes, 23 October 1799

Wack Broomhead
(Male) Born Over Haddon, Derbyshire, c.1848
(Haddon, Derbyshire, 1851 census)

Emily Pocohontas [*sic*] Brown
Born Gravesend, Kent, 1847
An appropriate middle name: native American princess
Pocahontas, wife of English colonist John Rolfe and star of the Disney
animated film, died in Gravesend 230 years earlier.

Irony Thomas Brown
Born Romford, Essex, 1843

Nimrod Buckett
Born Portsmouth, Hampshire, 1820

Content Increase Buckley
Born Oldham, Lancashire, 1860

Benito Mussolini Buckross
Born np 1932; died Bradford, Yorkshire, 1997
*What may have sounded like an interesting choice of first names
when the fascist dictator was allegedly making the Italian trains run
on time perhaps seemed less appealing ten years later.*

Lovely Budge
Born Chard, Somerset, 1881

Alefounder Bugg
Born Brantham, Suffolk, 18 April 1817

Original Bugg
Born Lincoln 1907

Lamentation Bullivant
Born Spilsby, Lincolnshire, 1841

Rahartha Bung
(Female) Born Tiverton, Devon, c.1860 (Newton Abbot, Devon, 1861 census)

Philemon Bungy
Born Brighton, Sussex c.1873 (Brighton, 1881 census)

Philadelphia Bunnyface
Laneast, Cornwall, will, 1722
*The inclusion of this name among those published by the Cornwall
Record Office in its list of 'Silly Names' upset some people called
Boniface, who believed the name to be a corruption of theirs.*

Bounce E. Burbidge
(Female) Born Sheffield, Yorkshire, c.1856 (Sheffield, 1871 census)

Furry Jane Burbidge
Born Friskney, Lincolnshire, c.1847 (Friskney, 1871 census)

Rhoda Failing Burpee
Born Bucklow, Cheshire, 1905

Tim Burr
Born Watford, Hertfordshire, 1867

Ethelbert Bursting
Born Waterbeach, Cambridgeshire, c.1877 (Cambridge, 1901 census)

Judas Iscariot Burton
Born Stafford 1882

Wealthy Buscomb
Buried St Breock, Cornwall, 1723

Florence May Bust
Born Nottingham 1895

Thankful Butler
Born Hastings, Sussex, 1838

Providence Buttefant
(Female) Born np c.1806 (Southwold, Suffolk, 1841 census)

Delight Butterworth
Born np c.1856, Massachusetts, USA (Droylsden, Lancashire, 1891 census)

Leviathan Buttress
Born Stevenage, Hertfordshire, c.1853 (Bartlow, Cambridgeshire, 1881 census)

Bob By
Born Battle, Sussex, c.1841 (Battle, 1841 census)
*Along with names such as Er and Up, By is one of a small
number of two-letter surnames in the UK.*

—C—

Harie Cabaret
Baptized London 10 January 1628

William Snafu Cadman
Born St George, Southwark, London, 1853
*If correct, this would be a unique usage of 'Snafu' – better known as
the acronym for 'Situation Normal All Fucked Up' – as a name, but is
more probably a snafu by the Registrar, and is meant to be 'Snape'.*

Julia Caesar
Born Westminster, London, c.1832 (Lambeth, 1851 census)
Julia Caesar was the daughter of Octavius Caesar, a coachsmith.

Julius Caesar
Married Alice Dente, Mitcham, Surrey, 10 April 1596

Rose Cann Cann
Born Barnstaple, Devon, 1867

Peculiar Cannon
(Female) Born Claypole, Lincolnshire, c.1876
(Hawton, Nottinghamshire, 1881 census)

Mephibosheth Capstack
(Male) Born Halifax, Yorkshire, 1869
(Northowram, Yorkshire, 1871 census)

Truly Carbon
Born Dorking, Surrey c.1869
(Broadwater Down, Kent, 1901 census)

I. D. Card
(Female) Born Portsmouth,
Hampshire, 1908

Valentine Card
(Male) Born np 1913;
died Chelmsford, Essex, 1993

Joseph Greenhouse Careless
Born Walsall, Staffordshire, 1874

John Lucknow Hidden Carpenter
Born Upton-upon-Severn, Worcestershire, 1859
*His name presumably commemorated the Siege of Lucknow,
India, two years earlier.*

Clint Cartilige
Born Prescot, Lancashire, 1849

Splash Carver
Born np 1913; died Romsey, Hampshire, 2001

George Frisky Cattermole
Born Depwade, Norfolk, 1896

Swill Baden Dentwyford Cawthorne
Born Leeds, Yorkshire, c.1900 (Chapel Allerton, Yorkshire, 1901 census)

Mary Celeste
Born Lancashire c.1811 (Liverpool, Lancashire, 1841 census)
*A spookily prescient name – the mysterious case of the abandoned
ship* Mary Celeste *did not occur until 1872.*

Flora Sexburga Chambers
Born Durham c.1874 (Altrincham, Cheshire, 1881 census)

Moon Chaplin
Died Norwich, Norfolk, 1844

Molesbury Vim Chapman
(Male) Born Helpston, Northamptonshire, c.1847
(Newborough, Northamptonshire, 1871 census)

Eliza Kanbone Chegwidder
Baptized Feock, Cornwall, 28 May 1848

Alice Louisa Damp Child
Born Sandown, Hampshire, c.1877
(Portsea, Hampshire, 1891 census)

Charity Chilly
Baptized Menheniot, Cornwall, 24 November 1736

Emma Chiset
Born Brighton, Sussex, c.1828 (Brighton, 1851 census)

Ah Choo
Married Stepney, London, 1882

Jesus Christ
Born np 1940; died Rotherham, Yorkshire, 2004

Merry Christmas
Born Midhurst, Sussex, 1874

Sabbath Church
(Male) Baptized Wybunbury, Cheshire, 3 March 1731

El Cid
(Female) Baptized St Paul, Norwich, Norfolk, 25 April 1686

Minnie Pudentiana Clague
Born West Derby, Lancashire, 1872

George Edward Short Clampit
Born Newton Abbot, Devon, 1848

Charlotte Clapsaddle
Born np c.1796 (Rochdale, Lancashire, 1841 census)

Pussie Maude L. Clarke
Born Lexden, Essex, 1898

Argy Clatworthy
(Female) Born Exeter, Devon, 1876

Curvey Cleary
Born Newcastle upon Tyne, Northumberland, c.1846
(Paddington, London, 1891 census)

Minnehaha Clements
Born Wandsworth, London, 1874

Pubella Clements
(Female) Born Middlesex c.1879 (Lambeth, London, 1881 census)

Aureola Clinton
Born Battersea, London, c.1892 (Battersea, 1901 census)

Jelling Cluck
Baptized Bedlington, Northumberland, 17 December 1671

Jessie Clutterbuck Clutterbuck
Born Chepstow, Monmouthshire, 1845

Charles Cobweb
Baptized St James Roman Catholic Church, Winchester, Hampshire,
12 February 1818

Mary Ann Cocaine
Born Derbyshire c.1828 (Failsworth, Lancashire, 1901 census)

Earthy Cocksedge
Born Stowmarket, Suffolk, c.1899 (Stowmarket, 1901 census)

Christopher Cockshit
Baptized Clayton with Frickey, Yorkshire, 14 October 1771

Admonition Codd
Died Newton Abbot, Devon, 1842

Not Wanted James Colvill
Born Lambeth, London, 1861

William Conqueror
Born Sunderland, Durham, 1862

Norman Conquest
Born Lewisham, London, 1904

Ellen Slow Cooch
Born Northampton 1838

Harry Tantrum Cook
Born Stockbridge, Hampshire, 1894

Humiliation Cook
Died Ipswich, Suffolk, 1848

Sexy Cook
Died Bedminster, Somerset, 1848

William Henry Boke Cool
Baptized St Andrew by the Wardrobe, London, 5 April 1856

Honey Coombs
Born Stratford-upon-Avon, Warwickshire, 1880

Richard Transvestent Copp
Born np 1910; died Carlisle, Cumberland, 1995

Charles Crusher Corale
Born Leicester 1844

Henry Porn Cordery
Born Petersfield, Hampshire, 1872

Chunky Cornfield
Born np 1931; died Birmingham, West Midlands, 2000

T. Cosy
(Male) Born South Molton, Devon, c.1820 (South Molton, 1881 census)

Flake Cox
(Female) Born Hampshire c.1891 (Battersea, London, 1891 census)

Knickless J. Cox
(Male) Born Liverpool, Lancashire, c.1877 (Liverpool, 1881 census)

Lurking Crabb
Born Gosfield, Essex, c.1780 (West Hanningfield, Essex, 1861 census)

Charlotte Crack
Married John Amos, St Leonard, Shoreditch, London, 11 October 1846

Irene May Crack
Born Bury St Edmunds, Suffolk 1913; died 1989

Patience Creep
Baptized Boyton, Cornwall, 3 October 1790

Peter Creeper
Baptized Tresmeer, Cornwall, 7 August 1768

Edmund Crisp Crick Crick
Born Loddon, Norfolk, 1842

Lusty Gladstone Cripps
Born Highworth, Wiltshire, 1894

Soapy Crooks
Married Bosmere, Suffolk, 1891

Chris Cross
Born Trull, Somerset, 1 November 1598

Orlando Furiosa Cross
Buried St Mary, Lichfield, Shropshire, 5 April 1621

Fuxilla Crowther
(Female) Born Facit, Lancashire, c.1829
(Whitworth, Lancashire, 1871 census)

Cosmo Crump
Born Pimlico, London, c.1863 (Islington, 1901 census)

Salome Cruncher
Born Stratford, Nottinghamshire, c.1841
(Newington, London, 1881 census)

George Sidney Crush Crush
Born Chelmsford, Essex, 1845
and
George Sidney Crush Crush
Born Cheltenham, Gloucestershire, 1845
Both boys were born in the same year and given the same unusual combination of names.

Economy Joseph Cumpston
Born Brixworth, Northamptonshire, 1878

Ethel Nastina Cundick
Born Warminster, Wiltshire, 1877

Philliane Cunnilli
Born Birmingham, Warwickshire, 1905

T. Cupp
(Female) Born Beaminster, Dorset, 1876

Cornelius Curse
Baptized Leake, Lincolnshire, 19 May 1664

Margaret Curvy
Baptized Rampton, Cambridge, 16 September 1627

—D—

Diddy Daddilums
(Female) Born Hertfordshire c.1874 (St Albans, Hertfordshire, 1881 census)

Pubella Dalt
Born Stockport, Cheshire, c.1840 (Stockport, 1861 census)

Robert Morris Dancer
Born Prescot, Lancashire, 1903

Fuchny Mottieve Dangerfield
Married Newington, London, December 1850

Dann Dangle
Married Uxbridge, Middlesex, 1857

Admonish Daniel
(Female) Born Cramlington, Northumberland, c.1871
(Cramlington, 1881 census)

Dansey Dansey
(Male) Baptized St Helen's, Worcester, 18 September 1800

William Mikado Danvers
Born Liverpool, Lancashire, 1886
Gilbert & Sullivan's comic opera The Mikado *had opened
in London on 14 March 1885.*

Agnes Cigarette Danyow
Born Raglan, Monmouthshire, c.1865
(Tafolwern, Monmouthshire, 1891 census)

William Cupid Dart
Born np c.1843; died Bristol, Gloucestershire, 1903

Anchorite Peacock Davies
Born Ruthin, Denbighshire, 1837

Thomas Tricky Davies
Born np c.1844; died St George Hanover Square, London, 1887

William Quack Dawson
Born Tynemouth, Northumberland, 1872

Name the Day

Any Day
Born Barningham, Suffolk, c.1857
(Crawshawbooth, Lancashire, 1871 census)

Christmas Day
(Male) Baptized Lowestoft, Suffolk, 27 December 1762

Godfrey Armistice Day
Born np 11 November 1923*;
died Milton Keynes, Buckinghamshire, 2003

Lucky Day
Born Blything, Suffolk, 1859

May Day
Died Axbridge, Somerset, 1842

Selby Day
Born Ashton-under-Lyne, Lancashire, 1897

Time Of Day
(Male) Born Hoo, Kent, 1899

Valentine Day
Born Leeds, Yorkshire, 1842

Winter Day
Born Romsey, Hampshire, 1845

Earwacker Deadman
Born Alton, Hampshire, 1849

Erneburga De Flamville
Wife of Hugh De Hastings, born Bordwell, Leicestershire, 1109

Edmond Sufferrer De Mullett
Married Bolton, Lancashire, 1898

Mystic May Dent
Born Halifax, Yorkshire, 1894

✌🏵❧

The fifth Armistice Day

Euphrasia De Spurtes
Born St Martin's, London, c.1838 (St Martin's, 1871 census)

Everleaner Dethick
Born Nottinghamshire c.1825 (Nottingham, 1841 census)

Charles Glue Dibley
Born Westhampnett, Sussex, 1885

Straddling Ernest E. Didot
Born Epsom, Surrey, 1900

Bill Ding
Baptized Easton-on-the-Hill, Northamptonshire, 22 September 1661

Ding Ding
Died Thanet, Kent, 30 April 1971

Warwick Giddy Dingle
Born np c.1821; died Plymouth, Devon, 1877

Lula Dingledine
Born Widdrington, Northumberland, 24 February 1872

Delaviveve Discipline
Born Pakenham, Suffolk, 1737

Thomas Dodgem
Baptized Great Edstone, Yorkshire, 3 October 1774

Melcom [sic] Garabed Donabed
Married Liverpool, Lancashire, 1906

All Done
Born Derby 1898

Prudentia Doolittle
Born np c.1852; died Ormskirk,
Lancashire, 1906

Ben Dover
Baptized St George in the East, London,
10 March 1839

Eileen Dover
Born np 1924; died Swindon, Wiltshire, 1987

Win Dow
Born Maldon, Essex, 1886

Ida Down
Born Okehampton, Devon, 1894

Abishag Doxey
(Female) Died Ashbourne, Derbyshire, 1854

Anonyma Drane
Born Dunmow, Essex, 1893

Frederick Hair Driver
Born Glanford Brigg, Lincolnshire, 1898

Mesmer Dumbrell
Born Brighton, Sussex, 1871

Domingo Dumdum
Baptized Kirk Merrington, Durham, 4 September 1706

Dinah Dump
Born Whitechapel, London, 1897

Trulove Dunk
Born Sheffield, Yorkshire, 1 January 1870

Hugh Dunnet
Born Scotland c.1836 ('attendant to the insane',
Dinsdale Asylum, Dinsdale, Durham, 1861 census)

I. Dunnit
(Female) Born Paisley, Renfrewshire, 9 October 1812

No More Durrant
Born Risbridge, Suffolk, 1899

James Brook Dust Dust
Born St Pancras, London, 1841

Uriah Dust
Married Anne Comely, Kingston St Michael, Wiltshire, 8 October 1772

Barb Dwyer
Baptized Sacred Heart and English Martyrs, Thornley, Durham, 7 January 1877

Sexbus Dyball
Born Ludlow, Shropshire, c.1832; died Reigate, Surrey, 1898

Alfred Arthur Forsaken Dymock
Born Croydon, Surrey, 1862

—E—

Emmeline Nirvana Eaborn
Born Wrexham, Denbighshire, 1902

Gladys Rose Early
Born Wandsworth, London, 1899

Epenetus Earwaker
• Born St Saviour, Southwark, London, 1871

Epaphreditus Eatty
(Male) Born St Luke, Middlesex, c.1830 (St Luke, 1881 census)

Cliff Edge
Born Haslingden, Lancashire, 1903

Oracabessa Edge
Baptized Little Ryburgh, Norfolk, 10 November 1862

Esther Egg
Married Glanford Brigg, Lincolnshire, 1863

National Elder
Born South Shields, Durham, c.1864 (South Shields, 1881 census)

Finale Eldridge
Born Wharfedale, Yorkshire, 1893

Kate Breeder Elliott
Born Playden, Sussex, c.1854 (Rye, Sussex, 1861 census)

Alice Nut Brown Emmett
Born Leeds, Yorkshire, 1864

Albina Gubbing Enticknap
Baptized Chertsey, Surrey, 20 January 1833

Ann Eraser
Married John Mackie, Aberdeen, 13 May 1831

Augustus Caesar Evans
Born Bedwelty, Monmouthshire, 1874

F. Ewe
(Male) Married St Pancras, London, 1899

Worthy Extra
Married Malmesbury, Wiltshire 1865

—F—

Job Fab
(Male) Married Elizabeth Banyard, Teversham,
Cambridgeshire, 6 April 1713

Eva Faithfull
Born Winchester, Hampshire, 1895

Madora Fankboner
(Female) Born Wales c.1861 (Claines, Worcestershire, 1861 census)

Ancient Fanthorpe
(Male) Born Lincoln 1843 (Kingston upon Hull, Yorkshire, 1881 census)

Sidney Hilarious Farrow
Born St Marylebone, London, 1877

Drusilla National Fear
Born Axbridge, Somerset, 1896

Jemima Lottery Fearman
Born Holborn, London, 1852

Orgie B. Feast
(Female) Born Fareham, Hampshire, c.1879
(Fareham, 1881 census)

Wave Feather
(Male) Born Windsor, Berkshire, c.1825
(Hampton, Middlesex, 1851 census)

Obediencia Feck
Baptized Poundstock, Cornwall, 12 March 1642

Low Fee
Married Chorlton, Cheshire, 1908

Number Seven Fell
Born Alton, Hampshire, 1879

Ethel Congress Few
Born Chesterton, Cambridgeshire, 1904

Ffaithfull Ffillips
Married Lanreath, Cornwall, 29 November 1660

Fickess Fickess
Born Chesterton, Cambridgeshire, 1844

Fried Field
Married East Preston, West Sussex, 1890

Paddy Fields
Born West Derby, Lancashire, 1908

Benny Fitt
Born Shoreditch, London, 1876

Sarah Ann Flapper
Born Gateshead, Durham, c.1876 (Gateshead, 1881 census)

Joseph Flicker Flicker
Born Dartford, Kent, 1844

Egesta M. Flopsey
(Female) Born Romford, Essex, c.1870 (Romford, 1871 census)

Albert Fluck Fluck
Born Westbury-on-Severn, Gloucestershire, 1893

Fanetta Annie Fluke
Born Melksham, Wiltshire, 1867

Wonderful George Forsdyke
Born Bosmere, Suffolk, 1886

Sally Forth
Born Eye, Northamptonshire, c.1847 (Eye, 1881 census)

Ellen Step Forward
Born East Stonehouse, Devon, 1846; died Penzance, Cornwall, 1848

George Tweet Foster
Born Mattingley, Hampshire, c.1870 (Heckfield, Hampshire, 1891 census)

Scott Free
Born Bethnal Green, London, 1901

Al Fresco
Born St Giles, London, 1853

Dresden China Fretwell
Born Wortley, Yorkshire, 1880

Gladys Friday
Born np 1900; died Brent, Middlesex, 1987

Catherine Frisky
Born np c.1826; died Uppingham, Rutland, 1907

Hopton Frothingham
Baptized St Andrew, Holborn, London, 14 January 1657

William Gubb Fry Fry
Born Barnstaple, Devon, 1852

Bathiah Fumble
Married John Miller, St Katherine by the Tower, London, 16 November 1729

Sweetie Winifred Futter
Born Blofield, Norfolk, 1898

—G—

Christina Rebecca Gagging
Born St George, Southwark, London, 1862

Isabella Blows Gale
Born Greenwich, Kent, 1837

Opportune Ganwit
(Female) Born France c.1842 (Shirburn, Oxfordshire, 1871 census)

Phil Gapp
Married Forehoe, Norfolk, 1859

Medium Matilda Garlick
Born Melksham, Wiltshire, 1860

Pearly Gates
Married Kevin M. Cadle, Westminster, London, 1996

Fartune Gathercole
(Female) Born Norfolk c.1766 (Mattishall, Mitford, Norfolk, 1841 census)

Skimpool Gealy
Born Leeds, Yorkshire, c.1880 (Armley, Yorkshire, 1901 census)

Forget-me-not Geeves
Born Hertford 1898

Ann Clown Gentleman
Married St Pancras, London, 1880

Big George
Died Guisborough, Yorkshire, 1871

Lolita Stuckey Gifford
Born Llandilofawr, Carmarthenshire, 1882

John Giggler
Born Luton, Bedfordshire, c.1826 (Biggleswade, 1861 census)

John Farmer Giles
Born np c.1881; died Witney, Oxfordshire, 1904

Glamour Girl
Married Robert H. Travers, Edmonton, London, 1960

Peter Gloob
Married Elizabeth Natters, Chester-le-Street, Durham, 23 June 1716

Fynae Glue
Baptized Pateley Bridge, Yorkshire, 16 April 1634

Margaret Glug
Baptized Brechin, Angus, 20 May 1756

George Goblin
Married Maria Boot, Whorlton, Yorkshire, 11 June 1805

Blastus Godley
Married Alicia Seabrooke, St Stephens, St Albans, Hertfordshire,
21 November 1609

Herrman [*sic*] Goering
Born Birmingham, Warwickshire, 1880

Lactarias Golley
Born Caerhays, Cornwall, c.1846 (Caerhays, 1851 census)

Finess Gollop
Born Poole, Dorset, 1857

Alexander Gonk
Baptized Arbroath, Angus, 18 June 1810

Simeon Goo
Baptized St Michael, Ashton-under-Lyne, Lancashire, 24 August 1828

Old England Goodson
Born Aylesbury, Buckinghamshire, 1875

Alonzo Goody Goody
Born Sudbury, Suffolk, 1856

Mary Strip Gordon
Born Poplar, London, 1864

Manly Gore
Born Brighton, Sussex, c.1863 (Portsea, Hampshire, 1871 census)

Gertrude May Gotobed
Born Wandsworth, London, 1900

Waxwax Goughe
Baptized Burrington, Herefordshire, 23 January 1561

One Too Many Gouldstone
Born West Ham, Essex, 1870

Isobel Gowdielock
Married James Dunn, Peebles, 25 September 1756

Anna Gram
Born np c.1811 (Ambrosden, Oxfordshire, 1841 census)

Errata Grant
Born Sheffield, Yorkshire, 1844

Jane Trafalgar Grapes
Born Newport, Isle of Wight, 1805
One of the children of John and Hannah Grapes, who were all given middle names that related to the Napoleonic Wars, including William Nile Grapes (1815), Charlotte Waterloo Grapes (1815) and Charles Wellington Grapes (1811).

George Grassmuck
Born Littlehampton, Sussex, c.1840
(Littlehampton, 1851 census)

Ann Gravity
Married Daniel Arnold, St Dunstan, Stepney, 28 September 1788

Contents Increase Greatorix
(Female) Born Oldham, Lancashire, 1872

Greatwichnellie May Greatwich
Born Ashton-under-Lyne, Lancashire, 1910

Barbary Groat
Baptized Westray, Orkney, 30 May 1808

Hephzibah Gromit
Married Boston, Lincolnshire, 1855

Ice Groom
Born Stockton-on-Tees, Durham, 1871

Sarah Grunge
Born St Marylebone, London, c.1818
(St George Hanover Square, London, 1851 census)

Tommy Gun
Born Evesham, Worcestershire, 1838

Fried Gunly
Born Lincoln 1838

—H—

Caractacus L. Habakkuk
Born np c.1857 (Peterstone Super Montern, Glamorgan, Wales 1881 census)

Angel Hackabout
(Male) Baptized St Luke, Old Street, Finsbury, London, 20 September 1752

Kink Hailagman
Married Liverpool, Lancashire, 1878

Gabriel Hairbottle
Baptized St Andrew by the Wardrobe, London, 20 August 1721

Trannie Percy Hampshire
Born Chertsey, Surrey, c.1897 (Chertsey, 1901 census)

Peter Handsomebody
Baptized St Andrew, Holborn, London, 19 February 1758

Rifle Handworker
Born Russia c.1851 (Leeds, Yorkshire, 1891 census)

Beniventrus Hanky
'Drowned while bathing at Le Posterne', Chester, 6 August 1586
(Chester Coroners' Inquests)

Robert Jackson Hardcore
Born Long Preston, Yorkshire, c.1842
(Henllan, Denbighshire, 1881 Wales census)

Abort Hardman
Born Oldham, Lancashire, c.1860 (Oldham 1861 census)

Bartelmowe Hardup
Married Margaret Sewell, Smallburgh, Norfolk, 15 November 1601

Hannah Harmless
Married James Eston, Byford, Herefordshire, 13 October 1829

William No. 1 Harris
Married Islington, London, 1896

William No. 2 Harris
Married Maria A. Trent, Islington, London, 1913

Phil Harrup
Born Royston, Hertfordshire, 1839

Tom Dick Harry
Born Carmarthen 1890

Sweet Hart
Died St Mary Newington, London, 1837

Beaten Shakerley Harvey
Married Penzance, Cornwall, 1854

Henry Hatful
Died Holborn, London, 1908

Tom A. Hawk
Born St Dennis, Cornwall, c.1890 (St Dennis, 1891 census)

Neglected Heaks
Baptized St Mary's, Aylesbury, Buckinghamshire, 3 February 1627
The parish record also states: '1627 – Buried Neglected,
the daughter of Jeffrey Heaks, the 11th of February, and she was
so named because she had no God father or God mother
prepared at the time of Baptizing.'

Fluffy Heaver
Born np 1901; died Kensington and Chelsea, London, 1998

O. Heck
(Male) Born Leeds, c.1836
(Headingley cum Burley, Yorkshire, 1901 census)

O. Hell
(Male) Baptized Old Meeting Gaol Street Presbyterian, Great Yarmouth,
Norfolk, 24 February 1709

Snobia Hemp
(Female) Born Merther, Cornwall, c.1839 (Merther, 1851 census)

Agnes Skid Henderson
Born Scotland c.1831 (Earsdon, Northumberland, 1881 census)

Alpha and Omega Heydinrych
(Twins) Born Wandsworth, London, 1886

Xpopher Hic
Baptized Snaith, Yorkshire, 19 January 1607

Radium Hickie
Born Wandsworth, London, 1904

Exodus Hickling
(Female) Born Ripley, Derbyshire, c.1791 (Shillington, Yorkshire, 1861 census)

Thomas Antique Hicks
Born Cardiff, Glamorgan, 1852

Girly Hind
Born Southwell, Nottinghamshire, 1873

James Desperate Hines
Born Samford, Suffolk, 1885

Abraham and Joe Hitler
(Twins) Born Prestwich, Lancashire, 1901

Adolf Hitt
Born Germany c.1871 (Willesden, London, 1901 census)

B. Hive
Married Thomas Redding, Stepney, London, 17 August 1656

Gulielinus Hobbit
(Male) Married Margaretam [sic] Rayer, Swindon, Gloucestershire, 22 July 1607

Vage Hoke
(Male) Born Lettaford, Devon, c.1836 (Bridgewater, Somerset, 1901 census)

May Holiday
Born Westminster, London, 1878

Glossy Agnes Holland
Born Wooton St Lawrence, Hampshire, 1891

Mary Perpetual Homer
Born Blandford, Dorset, 1853

Honesty Honesty
(Male) Born Greenwich, Kent, c.1849 (Dover, Kent, 1891 census)

Harriet Fecund Hooper
Born Bethnal Green, London, 1848

Abacuck Hoore
Married Joan Wallpoole, Bury St Edmunds, Suffolk, 1575

Mary Crack Hopkins
Born Cardiff, Glamorgan, 1841

Jeronimo Hornblow
Married Mary Mew, Upton-cum-Chalvey,
Buckinghamshire, 1 October 1743

Adeline Louisa Maria Horsey de Horsey
Born London 24 December 1824;
died Corby, Northamptonshire, 25 May 1915

Hugh Gentleman Horspole
Born Wisbech, Cambridgeshire, 1900

Chastity Ellen Hosegood
Born St George, Southwark, London, 1844

Cautious House
Born Farnborough, Hampshire, 1859

Happy Helen Hovel
Born Flegg, Norfolk, 1851

Annie How
Born Ecclesfield, Yorkshire, 1843

Ernest William Gnash Hoyle
Born St Mary le Wigford, Lincoln, c.1872 (Lincoln, 1881 census)

Caiusillarcius Coriolanus Hubble
Married Lewisham, London, 1863

Pontius Pilate Hughes
Born Dewsbury, Yorkshire, 1872

Sexas Huish
Born Axbridge, Somerset, 1888

Penitent Humphreys
Married Manchester, Lancashire, 1850

Pleasure Hunter
(Female) Born Shipdham, Norfolk, c.1840 (Shipdham, 1851 census)

Napoleon Austin Lucas Hymen Hurry
Born Linton, Cambridgeshire, 1844

Alice Surprise Hutchinson
Born Islington, London, 1883

George Execellent [*sic*] Sargent Banning Hyne
Born Stoke Damerel, Devon, 1843

—I—

Dorothea Mary A. E. Iceberg
Born City of London 1873

Gabriel Incarnation
Married St George Hanover Square, London, 1855

Ann Inch
Baptized St Kew, Cornwall, 16 February 1713

F. Ing
(Male) Baptized Blean, Kent, 21 June 1829

F. Ingood
Born Tutbury, Staffordshire, c.1851
(Burton upon Trent, Staffordshire, 1861 census)

Kissey Inwards
Born Woburn, Bedfordshire, 1873

Cadwalader Ish
Born Llanbeblig, Caernarvonshire, c.1851 (Llanbeblig, 1851 Wales census)

—J—

Frothy Jackson
(Female) Born Markington, Yorkshire c.1831
(Potternewton, Yorkshire, 1901 census)

Question James
Born Williton, Somerset, 1880

Adolphus Shaft Jarman
Born Westminster, London, 1849

Offspring Jeeves
Born Biggleswade, Bedfordshire, 1876

Prodigal Robert Jennings
Born Battersea, London, 1858 (Battersea, 1861 census)

Jane Jiffy
Died South Shields, Durham, 1857

Rarely John
(Male) Born Cardiff, Glamorgan, c.1852 (Cardiff, 1861 census)

Miracle Johnson
(Female) Married Andrew Pratt, Hertford, c.1558

Keeping up with the Joneses

Decimal Jones
Born Corwen, Denbighshire, 1889

Frederick Alphabet Jones
Born Kendal, Westmorland, 1873

Lama Dana Jones
(Female) Born Cemmes, Montgomeryshire, c.1859
(Brynuchel, 1861 Wales census)

Robert Meteor Jones
Born Camberwell, London, 1857

Youthful Jones
Baptized St Andrew, Enfield, Middlesex, 29 May 1776

Starbuck Jordan
Born Market Bosworth, Leicestershire, 1874

Thankful Joy
(Female) Born Arundel, Sussex, 4 November 1816

Marathon Mary Judge
Born np 1909; died Chiltern, Buckinghamshire, 1999

Thomas Highfield Jump
Born Chorley, Lancashire, 1902

—K—

Wong Kee
(Female) Born China c.1874
(aboard ship *Glenlochy*, Middlesbrough, Yorkshire, 1901 census)

Christmas Evan Keel
Married Toxteth Park, Lancashire, 1894

Sargassa Zulu Kerrison
Born np c.1874; died Colchester, Essex, 1879

Indiana Kettle
Born Dudley, Staffordshire, 1854

Edwin King Key
Born Warwickshire c.1869 (Congleton, Cheshire, 1881 census)

Kings Rule

Ada Waste King
Born Worcester c.1860 (Lewisham, London, 1901 census)

Dirty King
Died Hatfield, Hertfordshire, 1863

Fay King
Born np 1922; died Bromley, Kent, 1998

Hopeful King
Born Norwich, Norfolk, 1866

Lee King
(Female) Born Chard, Somerset, c.1877
(North Wraxall, Wiltshire, 1861 census)

Matilda Handsomebody King
Married Barton Regis, Gloucestershire, 1893

Royal King
Born Portsmouth, Hampshire, 1902

Win King
(Female) Born Lancashire, c.1839
(Manchester, Lancashire, 1841 census)

Harriet Circus Kirby
Born Skipton, Yorkshire, 1904

Edmund Stanley Knife
Born City of London 1892

Pleasant Knight
(Female) Born Blaxhall, Suffolk, c.1781 (Blaxhall, 1861 census)

Tamara Knight
Born np c.1882; died Aston, Warwickshire, 1892

Mary Immaculate Knox
Born Merthyr Tydfil, Glamorgan, 1909

Industrious Kubb
Born Chelsea, London, c.1806 (Wandsworth, London, 1881 census)

Pock Kum
Born np c.1854; died Holyhead, Anglesey, 1894

—L—

Easter Ladle
Married John Spalding, St Augustine, Norwich, Norfolk, 31 March 1793

Appolonia Lallas
(Female) Born np c.1801 (Powick, Worcestershire, 1841 census)

Panter Lambert
Married Wellingborough, Northamptonshire, 1912

Dowsabell Lambole
(Female) Married William Boles, St Swithun over Kingsgate,
Winchester, Hampshire, 19 July 1624

Leonard Level Land
Born Wisbech, Cambridgeshire, 1900

Bona Large
Died Freebridge Lynn, Norfolk, 1850

Fishy Larkar
Born Kent c.1815 (Greenwich, Kent, 1851 census)

Alice Lashings
Born Brighton, Sussex, c.1833 (Brighton, 1881 census)

Henery Zaphnath La Small
Born Dover, Kent, c.1822 (Carlby, Lincolnshire, 1851 census)

Laura Lather
Born Shardlow, Derbyshire, 1893

Ernest Laughter
Born Bromsgrove, Worcestershire, c.1880 (Bromsgrove, 1881 census)

Carnage Laverack
Born Selby, Yorkshire, 1877

Aymyn Electric R. Lawrence
Born Pontypridd, Glamorgan, 1908

Fling Lazewody
(Female) Born Stoke Fleming, Devon, c.1879 (Stoke Fleming, 1901 census)

Manish Leather
Born Walthamstow, Essex, c.1890 (Shirley, Hampshire, 1901 census)

Mabel Jubi Lee
Born Peterborough, Northamptonshire, 1897
Named as a patriotic tribute to Queen Victoria, who celebrated her Diamond Jubilee in this year.

Anaesthesia Leech
Born np 1903; died Hartlepool, Durham, 1903

Starlight D. V. Le Garde
Married William H. Jones, Llanrwst, Denbighshire, 1913

Lucinda Legassick Legassick
Born Penzance, Cornwall, 1874

Modern Leggo
Born Penzance, Cornwall, 1859

Fan Light
Baptized West Wittering, Sussex, 20 February 1760

Medium Light
Died Henley, Oxfordshire, 1849

Joseph Lightowlers Lightowlers
Born Bradford, Yorkshire, 1878

Hephzibah Lillycrap
Married Lesnewth, Cornwall, 22 September 1768

Phil Ling
Born St Olave, Southwark, London, 1882

Strange Livings
(Male) Born Little Hallingbury, Essex, c.1863 (Little Hallingbury, 1871 census)

Cautious Constance Lock
Born Binstead, Hampshire, c.1871 (Binstead, 1891 census)

Miles Long
Born Sleaford, Lincolnshire, 2 January 1661

Noah Lott
Baptized Hipswell, Yorkshire, 16 August 1843

True Love
Born Newington, London, 1848

George Conk Lovibond
Born East Chinnock, Somerset, c.1811 (East Chinnock, 1861 census)

Bea Lowe
Baptized Winwick, Lancashire, 18 Oct 1706

Skimer Lunce
Born Tonbridge, Kent, c.1869 (Wandsworth, London, 1891 census)

Copernicus Mephibosheth Lynam
Born Basford, Nottinghamshire, 1898

—M—

Charlotte Grease MacDonald
Born West Derby, Lancashire, 1877

Beaky Mace
Born np 1929; died Surrey 2001

Elizabeth Drizzle MacLean
Died St Luke, London, 1858

Veneril Virtue Maggs
Married Clifton, Gloucestershire, 1865

Major Major
Born Islington, London, 1871

Arthur Phosphor Mallam
Born Headington, Oxfordshire, 1872

Frou-Frou Mallett
Born np c.1904; died St Pancras, London, 1907

Dinonysius Mancarter
Married St Endellion, Cornwall, 30 July 1748

Prism Manchip
(Female) Born Bridgwater, Somerset, c.1810 (Bridgwater, 1851 census)

Charity Mangle
Baptized Chesterfield, Derbyshire, 28 January 1834

Phoebe Manhole
Married John Clarke, Peatling Magna, Leicestershire, 16 November 1835

Armageddon Danbury Margerum
Born East Stonehouse, Devon, 1875
(Raunds, Northamptonshire, 1881 census)

Zaphnaphpanth Marker
(Male) Born Nottingham c.1811 (Greasley, Nottinghamshire, 1841 census)

Thats Marshall
Born Walkeringham, Nottinghamshire, c.1881
(Normanby, Lincolnshire, 1901 census)

Polyphemus Ann Martin
Born Medway, Kent, 1903

Thomas Alias Christ Martin
Born Wiltshire c.1811 (Warminster, Wiltshire, 1841 census)

Panting Mary
(Female) Born Crockley, Wiltshire, c.1842 (Paddington, London, 1901 census)

Martha Masculine
Married Robert Marsh, St Katherine by the Tower, London, 18 November 1675

Hannah Mattress
Died Bishop Auckland, Durham, 1859

Patience Mayhem
Married William Vigian, Maidstone, Kent, 19 January 1596

Preserved McDonald
(Female) Born Elgin, Moray, c.1810 (Elgin, 1851 Scotland census)

Mercy Mee
(Female) Born Loughborough, Leicestershire, 1880

Minnie Mee
Born Derby 1873

A. Men
(Male) Born Cornwall c.1840 (Camborne, Cornwall, 1841 census)

O. Men
(Male) Born Blackfriars, London, c.1870 (Southwark, London, 1881 census)

Mary Mermaid
Baptized St Martin-in-the-Fields, London, 30 May 1690

Mildew Michaels
(Female) Born London c.1874 (Kensington, London, 1901 census)

Egbert Stark Midlane
Born Newport, Isle of Wight, 1849 (Newport, 1901 census)

Jane Whip Miller
Born Tynemouth, Northumberland, 1891

Arthur Mind
Born Poplar, London, 1907

Arthur Minute
Born Hastings, Sussex, 1882

Foam Mitchell
(Female) Born Tottenham, London, c.1866
(Hackney, London, 1891 census)

Lowdy Moan
Baptized Tywardreath, Cornwall, 4 November 1666

Harriet Moans
Baptized Enniskillen, Fermanagh, Ireland, 20 March 1865

Faithfull Mock
(Male) Married Elizabeth Cullis, Roche, Cornwall, 5 May 1702

Nelly Monk Monk
Born Bedwelty, Monmouthshire, 1886

Nelson Monument
Born Mitford, Norfolk, 1872

Phases of the Moon

Cyril Centurion Moon
Born np 1922; died Chippenham, Wiltshire, 1985

Mary Moon Moon
Born Clutton, Somerset, 1882

Nehemiah Epaphrodites Moon
Born Frome, Somerset, 23 February 1828

Robert Howling Moon
Born np c.1878; died Pickering, Yorkshire, 1882

Trash Moon
Born Kent c.1787 (Tenterden, Kent, 1851 census)

Zebulon Moon
Born Dudley, Staffordshire, 1860

Zipporah Moonshine
Born Mile End Old Town, London, 1908

Les Moore
Born np 1935; died Enfield, Middlesex, 2000

Lean Twister Morgan
Born Rhyl, Flintshire, c.1862 (Pensarn, Denbighshire, 1871 Wales census)

Charlotte Freezer Mortimer
Born Saffron Walden, Essex, 1879

Helen Naughty Morton
Born np 1906; died Hitchin, Hertfordshire, 1998

Libertine Moss
Married Ashton-under-Lyne, Lancashire, 1855

Reveille Naorose R. Motabhoy
Married Croydon, Surrey, 1892

Doris Large Mothers
Born Leicester 1899

Rocco Motto
Born Italy c.1854 (St Pancras, London, 1881 census)

Salome Mud
Born Mile End, London, c.1876 (Bethnal Green, London, 1891 census)

Henrietta Mug
Born Whitechapel, London, 1874

Margaret Muggle
Married William Prosser, St Mary Somerset,
London, 21 January 1627

Zealous Farraginous Mullard
Born Bedwelty, Monmouthshire, 1892

Ellis Wallis Mumpower
Born Wandsworth, London, c.1889 (Wandsworth, 1891 census)

Anne Muppet
Baptized St Nicholas, Brighton, Sussex, 12 October 1799

Magic Muxworthy
Born Doncaster, Yorkshire, 1889

—N—

Nancy Nappy
Baptized Hemingbrough, Yorkshire, 24 July 1785

Fish Pool Neville
Died Ongar, Essex, 1837

James Noose Newcomb
Born Newport, Monmouthshire, 1861

Martha Thunder Nipp
Born Hull, Yorkshire, c.1821 (Hull, 1851 census)

Alfred Nix Nix
Born Faversham, Kent, 1881

Munte Cum Bernet Nixon
Died Brampton, Cumberland, 1859

Harry Nobody
Born np c.1901; died Mile End Old Town, London, 1905

Hi Noon
(Male) Born Radford, Nottinghamshire, 1878

Zachary Noseworthy
Married Alice Dudeny, Dunchideock, Devon, 19 November 1699

Y. Nott
(Female) Born np 1930; died Tunbridge Wells, Kent, 2002

Rachell Nude
Married Stephen Smith, Caister-on-Sea, Norfolk, 20 November 1572

Ada Nudy
Married Harry Bott, Ecclesall Bierlow, Yorkshire, 1913

Priscilla Nuke
Married Edward Martyn, Cathedral Church of St Thomas of Canterbury,
Portsmouth, Hampshire, 18 April 1704

Uranus Nussey
Married Dewsbury, Yorkshire, 1890

Strop Willy Nutall
Born Higher Booths, Lancashire, c.1841 (Newchurch, Lancashire, 1861 census)

Nellie Hinge Nutt
Born Kensington, London, 1900

F. Off
(Male) Baptized Ampthill, Bedfordshire, 14 February 1875

Driphena Old
Born Stepney, London, 1849

Harold Snarl Oliphant
Born Salford, Lancashire, 1886

John Opium
Baptized St Andrew, Holborn, London, 5 May 1764

Rick O'Shea
Married Kennington, London, 1864

Ann Other
Died Leyburn, Yorkshire, 1899

Ephraim Very Ott
Born Plumstead, London, c.1879 (Plumstead, 1881 census)

George Special Ottaway
Born West Ham, Essex, 1873

Pluto Oulton
Born Manchester, Lancashire, 1871

Zechariah Outrage
Baptized Ryarsh, Kent, 6 August 1780

Fanny Overland
Born Wisbech, Cambridgeshire, 1876

Crispy Ann Overton
Born Lincolnshire, c.1876 (Wainfleet St Thomas, Orby,
Lincolnshire, 1841 census)

—P—

Knob Hill Palmer
Born Uppingham, Rutland, 1905

Matilda Panter-Downes
Died Bristol, Gloucestershire, 1901

Wal Paper
Born Greenwich, Kent, c.1864 (Greenwich, 1901 census)

Agape Parker
(Female) Born Oxford c.1875 (Oxford, 1891 census)

Blandina Parody
Born Bedwelty, Monmouthshire, 1875

Edwin Titanic Pascoe
Born np 1912; died Penzance, Cornwall, 1996
He was born twelve days before the Titanic *disaster, but
presumably named to commemorate its launch.*

Emily Odd Paste
Married West Ham, Essex, 1882

George Yokel Pavett
Born Leighton Buzzard, Bedfordshire, c.1874
(on ship *Pembroke*, Chatham, Kent, 1901 census)

Scunt Pazney
(Male) Born Kent c.1803 (Stone, Kent, 1841 census)

Faith Hope Charity Peace
Born Ashby-de-la-Zouch, Leicestershire, 1864

Ann Shakes Peare
Born Wrexham, Denbighshire, c.1849 (Wrexham 1901 census)

Easy Pease
Died Billericay, Essex, 1889

Nimby Pedder
Born West Derby, Lancashire, 1875

Acts Apostles Pegden
Born Dunkirk, Kent, c.1796 (Canterbury, Kent, 1851 census)

Cuthbert Penix
Born Mile End, London, c.1865 (Mile End, 1891 census)

Sexaple [sic] Pennell
Born Surrey c.1847 (Leamington Spa, Warwickshire, 1871 census)

Barbara Penthouse
Born Kirkby Malzead, Yorkshire, 5 October 1600

Talitha-Cumi People
Married Andover, Hampshire, 1852

Martha Ann Nark Perfect
Died Yarmouth, Norfolk, 1859

Perfect Perfect
Born Chatham, Kent, c.1887
(Chatham, 1891 census)

Boileta Perks
Born Birmingham, Warwickshire, 1843

Sue Perman
Born Wiltshire c.1791
(Downton, Wiltshire, 1841 census)

Sue Perrior
Married David Yeatman, Downton,
Wiltshire, 6 October 1755

Polly Hankey Phantom
Baptized St Nicholas, Liverpool, Lancashire, 31 January 1779

Sydgestermondayer Phillips
Married Thomas Jones, Shrewsbury, Shropshire, 1864
She was born in Shrewsbury in 1844 and said to have been baptized
Sigismunda Phillips, but when it came to her wedding no one,
including the bride, knew how to spell her name, so her marriage
was registered with this approximate phonetic version.

Sanspareil Audacious T. Philpott
Born Faversham, Kent, 1892

Hannah Grime Pickup
Born Oldham, Lancashire, 1860

Thomas Strangeways Pigg-Strangeways
Married Emily Dorothy Beck, Cambridge, 1902

Zankey Pilch
Married Mary Chapman, East Rudham, Norfolk, 7 January 1768

Narcissus Pinch
Born Shoreditch, London, 1860

Jane Curvey Pink
Born Bishop's Waltham, Hampshire, c.1835 (Bishop's Waltham 1891 census)

Arthur Pint
Born Portsmouth, Hampshire, c.1797 ('brewer', Portsea, 1851 census)

Darth Pish
Born Stoke-next-Guildford, Surrey c.1844 (Stoke-next-Guildford, 1851 census)

Frankensteine Pitt
Married Barton Regis, Gloucestershire, 1885

William Plank A. Plank
Born Poole, Dorset, 1886

Emma Nickers Platt
(Female) Born Hurst, Lancashire, c.1869 (Levenshulme, Lancashire, 1901 census)

Snowflake George Pledger
Born Hampstead, London, 1877

Howard Junie Ploof
Born Nottinghamshire c.1878 (Nottingham, 1891 census)

Richard Mayhem Pogson
Died Wisbech, Cambridgeshire, 1839

Lew Pole
Born Pontypridd, Glamorgan, 1898

May Pole
Born Leicester 1904

Caesar Policarp
Nantwich, Cheshire, will, 1692

Elias Pollymounter
Baptized St Stephen-in-Brannel, Cornwall, 14 March 1830
At the time of the 1851 census, there were fifteen Pollymounters,
all residing in the same parish; by 1871, there were four, all in
St Columb Major, Cornwall; now there are none.

Hannah Pong
Baptized Upton-cum-Chalvey, Buckinghamshire, 15 February 1818

Frayton Poocock
Born Laughton, Sussex, c.1825 (Chiddingly, Sussex, 1891 census)

Jean Pool
Born np c.1841; died West Derby, Lancashire, 1899

Harry Sequin Portch
Born Farnham, Hampshire, 1877

Wee Girlie Potter
Born Risbridge, Suffolk, 1906

Josephine Valkyrie A. Powell
Born Cardiff, Glamorgan, 1889
Wagner's Die Walküre *had been first performed in London in 1882.*

Tesco Power
(Female) Born Warwickshire c.1807 (Birmingham, 1841 census)

Burpee P. H. Preensides
(Male) Born Stallington, Lincolnshire, c.1864
(Middlesbrough, Yorkshire, 1871 census)

George Pregnant
Born np c.1830 (East Stonehouse, Devon, 1871 census)

Final Edwin Preston
(Male) Born Market Bosworth, Leicestershire, 1892
Final was, they hoped, the last-born of the six children of
Lot and Amy Preston.

The Price is Wright

High Price
Married Presteigne, Herefordshire, 1861

John Lower Price
Born Wolverhampton, Staffordshire, 1844

Mad Price
(Male) Born Bishop Auckland, Durham, c.1865
(Bishop Auckland, 1891 census)

Over Price
(Male) Born np c.1812 (Merthyr Tydfil, Glamorgan, 1841 census)

Silly Price
(Female) Born Sheffield, Yorkshire, c.1855 (Sheffield, 1891 census)

Worthy Price
Born Malmesbury, Wiltshire, 1857

Wright Price
Born Louth, Ireland c.1868
(Watford, Hertfordshire, 1871 census)

George Bambusy Primate
Baptized St Matthew, Bethnal Green, London, 17 October 1819

Jiggy Proper
(Female) Born Dowlais, Glamorgan, c.1840 (Dowlais, 1851 Wales census)

Arsenal Berriball Prout
Born Tavistock, Cornwall, 1845

Floppy Pryor
Died Ashton-under-Lyne, Lancashire, 1885

Joseph Ghost Puddephal
Born Coventry, Warwickshire, 1861

Bolthazer Puffparker
Baptized Crossthwaite, Cumberland, 29 January 1603

Fartumalus Purdger
(Male) Born Kent c.1829 (Margate, Kent, 1841 census)

—Q—

Edwin Mowgwong Quack
Married St Pancras, London, 1861

Pythagoras Quarry
Baptized St Pancras Old Church, London, 2 May 1847

B. Quick
(Female) Born Ireland c.1822 (Tower Hamlets, London, 1881 census)

Maude Quick Quick
Born Helston, Cornwall, 1878

—R—

Wacks Racke
(Male) Born Yorkshire c.1899 (Barnsley, Yorkshire, 1901 census)

Virgin Rackstraw
Died Wycombe, Buckinghamshire, 1896

Hiram Brown Rainwater
Born St Merryn, Cornwall, 9 October 1881

Thomas Thing Ramplin
Born Cosford, Suffolk, 1847

Nathaniel Ratcatcher
Married Amye Wright, Stoke-by-Nayland, Suffolk, 23 July 1622

Love Reading
Baptized Rickmansworth, Hertfordshire, 20 November 1768

Eva Ready
Born Halifax, Yorkshire, 1896

Violence Reason
Born Buckden, Huntingdonshire, c.1893 (Buckden, 1901 census)

Ethel Red
Born Kentish Town, London, c.1900 (St Pancras, London, 1901 census)

Sensitive Redhead
(Female) Born Bridlington, Yorkshire, 1873

Goblin Reeves
Born Orsett, Essex, 1848

John Estuary Register
Married Hastings, Sussex, 1874

Hughe Relief
Born Stackpole Elidor, Pembrokeshire, c.1579

Charlotte Rentfree
Born np c.1828; died Portsea Island, Hampshire, 1871

Francis Respect
Baptized Kirk Rushen, Isle of Man, 26 May 1793

Au Revoir
(Male) Born St Giles, London, 1887

August Revolt
Born np c.1836; died Northwich, Cheshire, 1894

Dusty Rhodes
Born np 1940; died Wigan, Lancashire, 1999

Yeah Rich
Born Devon c.1821 (Kingskerswell, Devon, 1841 census)

Irene Joy Riding
Born Preston, Lancashire, 1910

Isabel Ringer
Born Hartismere, Suffolk, 1911

Digory Ripper
Born Truro, Cornwall, 1870

Mike Robe
Baptized Kilsyth, Sterling, 15 May 1743

Marie Antoinette L. Robust
Married St Marylebone, London, 1905

High Rockett
Married Bridport, Dorset, 1856

Roger Roger
Baptized Moreton, Shropshire, 7 February 1587

Heavy Roots
Born Ryarsh, Kent, c.1823 (Cheshunt, Hertfordshire, 1871 census)

John Tight Roper
Born Guisborough, Yorkshire, 1898

Tommy Rot
Born Shoreditch, London, 1871

Fice Rotondo
Born Sunderland, Durham, c.1876 (Sunderland, 1901 census)

Susan Rottengoose
Baptized Hemsby, Norfolk, 10 July 1636

Roderick Random Round
Born np c.1814; died Blackburn, Lancashire, 1889

Catherine Roundabout
Married John Cook, St Martin, Birmingham,
Warwickshire, 29 December 1735

Dick Rubber
Born Bristol, Gloucestershire, 1838

Sudden Rusher
Born Keighley, Yorkshire, c.1847 (Keighley, 1851 census)

Grease Ellen Rushgrove
Born Gloucester 1861

Kenneth Creamy Russell
Born Lewisham, London, 1909

—S—

Pete Sake
Born Cheshire c.1840 (Macclesfield, Cheshire, 1841 census)

Gusty Sandbag
Born np c.1853; died Thornbury, Gloucestershire, 1902

Photo Gilbert Scales
Born Hartlepool, Durham, 1866

Susannah Scandal
Married James Musgove, Holy Trinity, Gosport, Hampshire,
26 December 1778

John Scared
Married Chester, Cheshire, 1892

Eliza Scavenger
Died Stepney, London, 1839

Hepsa Scoggins
(Female) Born Suffolk c.1830 (Badingham, Suffolk, 1841 census)

Zilpah Scotchedge
Baptized Rickmansworth, Hertfordshire, 20 June 1773

Timosin Scrag
Married James Oliver, Leek, Staffordshire, 25 October 1748

Isobella Scream
Baptized Paisley Abbey, Renfrewshire, 23 May 1824

Aaron Screech
Married Catherine Tippett, Saltash, Cornwall, 20 October 1746

Totty Seeds
Born St Olave, Southwark, London, 1885

C. Senor
(Male) Born Middlesex c.1831 (Clerkenwell, London, 1841 census)

Marmaduke Sewer
Married Mary Goulsbrough, St Paul, Lincoln, 11 June 1629

Huge Shakeshaft
Born Buerton, Cheshire, 1871 (Buerton, 1871 census)

Samuel Squelch Shakespeare
Born Ashby-de-la-Zouch, Leicestershire, 1841

Bertha Innerarity Shallcross
Born Wirral, Cheshire, 1877

Maria Shampoo
Baptized St Martin-in-the-Fields, London, 7 January 1664

Rick Shaw
Born Romford, Essex, c.1857 (Tottenham, London, 1881 census)

Nehemiah Shed
Born Rochford, Essex, 1852

Florry Shegog
Born Wolverhampton, Staffordshire, 1877

Loveless Shepherd
Died Thornbury, Gloucestershire, 1863

Methuselah Shonk
Died Romford, Essex, 1902

Hannah Quick Shugg
Born Penzance, Cornwall, 1852

I. Sickle
(Female) Born Newcastle upon Tyne, Northumberland, c.1857
(Washington, Durham, 1871 census)

C. Side
(Female) Born St Saviour, Southwark, London, 1841

I. Sight
(Female) Born Shirley, Hampshire, c.1895 (Shirley, 1901 census)

George Slaberdash
Born Bath, Somerset, c.1791 ('worm destroyer', Hereford, 1871 census)

Nutty Slack
Born Italy c.1864 (Islington, London, 1881 census)

James Scanty Slingsby
Born Hull, Yorkshire, 1840

Budgel Slop
Married John Mitchell, Bishops Cannings, Wiltshire, 18 June 1608

Tiny Slurd
(Male) Born Plymouth, Devon (Everton, Lancashire, 1881 census)

Sinderella [sic] Small
(Female) Born Cornwall c.1853 (Newton Abbot, Devon, 1881 census)

Didimus Smalley
Born Lincoln 1886

C. Letterquist Smither
(Male) Born Newington, Surrey, c.1839 (Greenwich, Kent, 1851 census)

George Zellweger Sneezum
Born Edinburgh, Midlothian, 4 July 1866

Selina Snip
Born West Ashford, Kent, 1846

Mary Snogglegrass
Born Fife c.1862 (St Giles-in-the-Fields, London, 1881 census)

Hargood Snooke
Married Ann Foote, Stoke Damerel, Devon, 11 April 1780

Arabella Snoot
Married Shaftesbury, Dorset, 1838

Eli Messiah Snutch
Born Birmingham, Warwickshire, 1878

Yetta Sofa
Born St George in the East, London, 1886

Sing Song
Died Liverpool, Lancashire, 1847

Mud Sowersby
Born Driffield, Yorkshire, 1879

Zenas Spaceman
Born Chesterton, Cambridgeshire, 1861

Shaga Spagatner
Died Holborn, London 1907

Sarah Mary Tumble Spargo
Born Newton Abbott, Devon, 1853

Ann Billion Sparkes
Married Shrewsbury, Shropshire, 1841

Ellinor Oil Spartalis
Born Tenby, Pembrokeshire, c.1870 (Tenby, 1871 Wales census)

Agabus Spendlove
Born Belper, Derbyshire, 1885

Spark Spinks
Born Thetford, Norfolk, 1840

Wilhelmina Tiffin Spirit
Born Hexham, Northumberland, 1901

Sidwella Splat
Married William Small, Chagford, Devon, 21 June 1613

John Spong Spong
Born Maidstone, Kent, 1842

Samuel Spoon
Married Anna Maria Aldred, St Peter Mancroft, Norwich,
Norfolk, 28 August 1858

Icy Constance Spragg
Born Fulham, London, 1904

Lettice Spray
Baptized Greasley, Nottinghamshire, 23 April 1633

Martin Spreadeagle
Married Elizabeth Pitcher, St Mary in the Marsh,
Norwich, Norfolk, 22 July 1672

Lezetta Stacker
Born Tynemouth, Northumberland, 1861

Focks Stain
(Male) Born Histon, Cambridgeshire, c.1807
(Great Gransden, Huntingdonshire, 1851 census)

Matilda Sperman Staines
Born Kensington, London, 1860

Silence Starbuck
Married Bingham, Nottinghamshire, 1841
*The surname 'Starbuck' is more commonly found in
Derbyshire and Leicestershire.*

Even Stephens
Born Llanwrthwl, Breconshire, c.1856
(Aberdare, Glamorgan, 1891 Wales census)

Grissell Stick
Married Hendrie Thomsoun [sic], South Leith, Midlothian, 8 July 1615

Joss Stick
Born Ulverston, Lancashire, 1887

Cornelius Sticky
Born Ireland c.1828 (Stepney, London, 1851 census)

Pharoah Stingemore
Born Axbridge, Somerset, 1875

Flint Stone
(Male) Baptized Marsham, Norfolk, 12 September 1790

Rosetta Stone
Baptized St Giles without Cripplegate, London, 3 August 1828
The Rosetta Stone was acquired by the British Museum in 1802.

Meleor Strangewidge
Buried Breage, Cornwall, 16 July 1620

Nicholas Streaker
Baptized St Oswald, Durham, 27 October 1747

Acheron Strench
Born Ireland c.1801 (Liverpool, Lancashire, 1841 census)
In Greek mythology, Acheron is one of five rivers of Hades.

Peculiar Stringer
Born np c.1803; died Wolverhampton, Staffordshire, 1882

Hercules Stuffing
Baptized Pleasley, Derbyshire, 1 December 1564

Dude Sugarberg
Born Mile End, London, c.1895 (Mile End, 1901 census)

Pubice Sula
(Female) Born Smethwick, Staffordshire, c.1816
(Harborne, Staffordshire, 1861 census)

Low Sum
Died Cardiff, Glamorgan, 1909

Martha Kitchen Sunshine
Born West Ham, Essex, 1868

Christian Sustenance
Baptized Attleborough, Norfolk, 10 January 1742

Er Sutcliffe
Born Lancashire c.1834 (Whalley, Lancashire, 1841 census)

Nanki Poo Sutton
(Male) Born Bristol, Gloucestershire, c.1887 (Bristol, 1891 census)

Mary Quato Swindle
Born Newcastle upon Tyne, Northumberland, 1902

Alphabeta Swithinbank
Died Hunslet, Yorkshire, 1849

Bamlet Neptune Switzer
Married Ada Charlotte Prince, Uckfield, East Sussex, 1890
Bamlet Neptune Switzer, later curate of Crowborough, Sussex,
was born at sea, hence his apt middle name.

Blender Swock
(Female) Born Dickleburgh, Norfolk, c.1832 (Diss, Norfolk, 1871 census)

Fare-well Sykes
Born Honley, Yorkshire, 1842
One of the four sons of Sydney and Betty Sykes,
Fare-well – who drowned in 1865 – was the brother of
Live-well, Do-well and Die-well Sykes.

Fortune Symons
(Female) Buried Hammersmith, London, 8 April 1723
She was claimed to be 111 years old.

—T—

Noah Tall
Baptized Antony, Cornwall, 21 April 1783

Mary Ann Lickerish Tandy
Born Warwick 1847

Ada Tantrum
Born Ludlow, Shropshire, 1875

Confucius Tarry
Born Leicester 1872

Dick Tater
Married Elizabeth Wayman, Elmore, Gloucester, 23 April 1621

Ann Teak
Ann, *née* Morley, married William Teak, Rothwell, Yorkshire, 22 May 1722

Thomas Teehee
Born Bilston, Staffordshire, c.1830 (Darlaston, Staffordshire, 1871 census)

Fannasibilla Temple
Baptized Sibbeston, Leicestershire, 24 May 1602

Tamper Tharth
Born Durham c.1838 (Bishop Wearmouth, Durham, 1841 census)

Hate Thatcher
Born Hungerford, Berkshire, 1848

Dick Thickbroom
Baptized Church Gresley, Derbyshire, 27 July 1718

A Few of My Favourite Things

Annie Thing
Born Broughton, Buckinghamshire, c.1870 (Broughton, 1891 census)
'Thing' is predominantly a Norfolk and Suffolk surname.

John Thomas Thing
Died Stow, Suffolk, 1872

Minnie Thing
Born Steeple Langford, Wiltshire, c.1888
(Steeple Langford, 1891 census)

Pleasance Thing
Born np c.1792; died Stow, Suffolk, 1869

Violet Thing
Born Ipswich, Suffolk, 1896

Silly Things
Born Stowmarket, Suffolk, c.1892 (St Peter, Suffolk, 1901 census)

William Thingy
Born Matlock, Derbyshire, c.1784 (Matlock, 1851 census)

James Bomb Third
Born Dundee, Forfarshire, c.1844 (Dundee, 1861 census)

Creamaleanouss Thompson
Married Liverpool, Lancashire, 1874

Old Book Thomspilie
Born Congleton, Cheshire, c.1863 (Hulme, Lancashire, 1871 census)

Nut Cell Nude Thorne
(Female) Born Ilminster, Somerset, c.1863 (Ilminster, 1901 census)

Albert Throbby
Born Leicester 1866

Hubert Revelation Thrower
Born Worksop, Nottinghamshire, 1905

Abraham Thunderwolff
Married Abigail Thomas, St Just-in-Roseland, Cornwall, 1813

Polly Tickle
Born Clifton, Lancashire, c.1876 (Swinton, Lancashire, 1901 census)

Sarah Tight Tight
Born Blofield, Norfolk, 1850

Frou-Frou Tilley
Born Bristol, Gloucestershire, c.1874
(Clifton, Gloucestershire, 1881 census)

Will Ting
Born Aldgate, London, c.1838 (City of London, 1891 census)

Experience Tingle
Married Thomas Meek, Walford, Herefordshire, 4 June 1689

Veginia [*sic*] Tiplady
Born Salford, Lancashire, c.1828 (Hulme, Lancashire, 1881 census)

Joseph Stalin Tipple
Born np 1942; died Dewsbury, Yorkshire, 1999

Ella L. Toadvine
Born Ryde, Isle of Wight, c.1882 (Surbiton, Surrey, 1901 census)

Thomas Toaster
Died Birmingham, Warwickshire, 1905

Vitruvius Palladio Toft
Married Alice Tatham, Barton-upon-Irwell, Lancashire, 1874

Extravaganza Muriel M. Tomkyns-Grafton
Born Ulverston, Lancashire, 1871

Beatrice Jester Toon
Born Chorlton, Lancashire, 1909

Onysephoris Toop
Married Christian Whisker, Seaton and Beer, Devon, 1 June 1708

Robert Ludolphus Davis Tosswill Tosswill
Born Newton Abbot, Devon, 1840

Clammy Townend
Born Pontefract, Yorkshire, c.1877 (Golcar, Yorkshire, 1891 census)

Martha Snowflake Tozer
Born Holywell, Flintshire, 21 January 1892

Benoni Trampleasure
Born Kingsbridge, Devon, 14 February 1815

Kate Trembler
Married Chorlton, Lancashire, 1892

Lucy Mysterious Trigg
Born Kensington, London, 1852

Halloween Lucy Troddan
Born Lanchester, Durham 1899

Vera Horsey Trott
Born Weymouth, Dorset, 1901

Misty Tuffin
Born Dorset c.1791 (Fontmell Magna, Dorset, 1841 census)

Ada Tugnutt
Born Steyning, Sussex, 1879

Merab Emily K. Jane Austen Tumber
Born Sheppey, Kent, 1860

Fridget Tumilty
Born Durham 1909

Page Turner
Born Axminster, Devon, 1865

Thomas Tweet
Died Tiverton, Devon, 1852

Mary Ann Twinkle
Baptized All Saints, Worcester, 26 December 1807

—U—

Fred Umbrella
Born Essex c.1875 (Danbury, Essex, 1881 census)

Elizabeth Underlay
Married Robert Baston, East Teignmouth, Devon, 10 February 1669

Volantine Unthank
Baptized Gateshead, Durham, 10 March 1717

Sapiens Upright
Married John Shergall, St Dunstan, Stepney, London, 9 April 1667

Alice Desideratum D. Upstill
Born Taunton, Devon, 1869

Rose Upward
Born Iwerne, Dorset, c.1847 (Motcombe, Dorset, 1871 census) .

Rosetta Vaculine
Born Hornchurch, Essex, c.1840 (Hornchurch, 1861 census)

Crucifix Valente
Died Sunderland, Durham, 1900

Nicholas Virgin
Born Guisborough, Yorkshire, 1875

Love Rake Vizard
Born Thornbury, Gloucestershire, 1892

German Voice
(Male) Married Elizabeth Watkins, Abbey Dore,
Herefordshire, 27 December 1731

Robert Blackadder Vuncombe
Born Chirnside, Berwickshire, c.1821 (Plumstead, London, 1881 census)

Gwendolen De Blois Wack
Born St Pancras, London, 1900

Xpofer Wad
Married Grace Murgatruid, Halifax, Yorkshire, 13 February 1552

Agrippa Wadge
Baptized Callington, Cornwall, 5 October 1750

Never Wait
Born Manchester, Lancashire, c.1834 (Warrington, Lancashire, 1891 census)

Isa Wake
(Female) Born North Shields, Durham, c.1863
(Gateshead, Durham, 1891 census)

Baby Walkers

Comfort Walker
(Female) Baptized Holbeck, Yorkshire, 29 June 1735

Jay Walker
(Female) Born Battersea, London, c.1889
(Hackney, London, 1901 census)

Pubus Walker
Born Bedale, Yorkshire, 1847

Risky Walker
Born Harrington, Cumberland, c.1880
(Parton, Cumberland, 1880 census)

Slack Walker
Born Wigton, Cumberland, 1840

Baxter Wall
Born West Ham, Essex, 1906

Bendy Wall
Born Yarmouth, Norfolk, c.1851 (Great Yarmouth, 1861 census)

Violent [*sic*] Irene Wallis
Born Barton Regis, Gloucestershire, 1883

Mary Bath Walters
Born Kingsbridge, Devon, 1854

Batman Wanless
Married Tynemouth, Northumberland, 1871

B. Ware
(Male) Born Pontypool, Monmouthshire, 1911

Luke Warm
(Female) Born Ely, Cambridgeshire, c.1891 (Ely, 1901 census)

Regula Warning
(Female) Born Middlesex c.1781
(St Mary Magdalen, Old Fish Street, London, 1841 census)

Libra Waterfall
(Female) Born Foleshill, Warwickshire, c.1803 (Foleshill, 1861 census)

Mary Blessed Waterfall
Born Holbeach, Lincolnshire, 1882

U. Watt
(Male) Married Castle Ward, Northumberland, 1900

Milky Wax
Born Yorkshire c.1806 (Wilberfoss, Yorkshire, 1841 census)

Harriet Moist Way
Born Newton Abbot, Devon, 1873

Mary Mallarkey Wealleans
Born Newcastle upon Tyne, Northumberland, 1904

Windebank Webb
Married Lambert Coot, St Margaret, Westminster,
London, 30 July 1668

Marvellous Webster
Married Todmorden, Yorkshire, 1861

George String West
Born Stepney, London, 1856

Adeline Wetnight
Born np c.1821 (St George Hanover Square, London, 1841 census)

Theseus Adonis Wexham
Born St George Hanover Square, London, 1883

Ferris Wheeler
(Male) Born Melksham, Wiltshire, 1860
*He predates the invention of the Ferris wheel (named after its
inventor George Washington Gale Ferris) by thirty-three years.*

Harriet Trickle Wheway
Married Nuneaton, Warwickshire, 1875

Christian Whinge
Baptized Great Barrington, Gloucestershire, 19 April 1590

Noah Whirligig
Buried Abdon, Herefordshire, 18 November 1813

Whiter than White

Albino White
Married Hackney, London, 1907

George Seamen White
Born Clifton, Gloucestershire, 1853

Nothing Henry White
Born Stoke-on-Trent, Staffordshire, 1852

Pearl E. White
Born Gravesend, Kent, 1908

Thomas Snow White
Born Frome, Somerset, 1882

Shirtliff Whitehead
Born Thorne, Yorkshire, 1904

Skyrack Whitham
Born Burnley, Lancashire, 1847

Rev Cornelius Whur
Born Pulham Market, Norfolk, 1782; died Loddon, Norfolk 1853
*In addition to his unusual name, Whur was regarded as one of the
worst poets of all time, penning verses with titles that included
'The Cheerful Invalid', 'The Diseased Legs' and 'The Armless Artist',
containing such immortal phrases as 'throbbing bosom' and
'whizzing balls'.*

Benjamin Loose Wick
Born Walsingham, Norfolk, 1846

Ralph Heavysides Wigham
Born np c.1844; died Teesdale, Durham, 1895

Lapidoth Stratton Wigley
(Female) Born Wallingford, Berkshire, 1846
*Lapidoth was the sister of Keturah, Philetus, Philiplus, Theophilius,
Tryphena and Tryphosa Wigley.*

George Sudden Willderspin
Born St Ives, Huntingdonshire, 1838

Something Willis
(Male) Born Ireland c.1801 (Glamorgan, Wales 1851 census)

Richard Edwards Windup
Born Burton upon Trent, Staffordshire, 1882

Ebenezer Hanshaw Winkie Winter
Born Norwich, Norfolk, 1841

G. Wiss
(Male) Born Whitechapel, London, 1865

Betsy Witch Witch
Baptized Ringwood, Hampshire,
1 September 1772

Lovelace Bigg Wither
(Male) Born Wymering, Hampshire, c.1806
(Wooton St Lawrence, Hampshire, 1841 census)

Careless Withers
Born Dudley, Staffordshire, 1859

Minnie Woman
Born Caistor, Lincolnshire, 1891

Ernest Womble Womble
Born Chesterfield, Derbyshire, 1908

Chip Wood
Born Huddersfield, Yorkshire, 1867

Juggler Woodhouse
Married Runcorn, Cheshire, 1884

Frederick Slick Woof
Born Kendal, Westmorland, 1885

Elkanah Wookey
Born Burrington, Somerset, c.1854 (Burrington, 1861 census)

Henry Clotworthy Woolcook
Born Penzance, Cornwall, 1859

Hot Mary Worth
Born Tavistock, Devon, 1867

Elizabeth Wrench Wrench
Born Ampthill, Bedfordshire, 1842

Olive Quatorzieme Wright
Born Stoke Damerel, Devon, 1897

Zownds Wright
Born Bedfordshire c.1781 (Harold, Bedfordshire, 1841 census)

Henry Wuss
Married St Pancras, London, 1902

Win Wynn
Born Prescot, Lancashire, 1889

—Y—

Humphredo Yallop
Baptized Hargham, Norfolk, 26 August 1672

Matthew Yellow Yellow
Born Thirsk, Yorkshire, 1862

Winifred Kate Yob
Baptized St Mary, Bristol, Gloucestershire, 26 May 1891

B. Yond
(Male) Born Prescot, Lancashire, 1905

Arden Thicknesse V. Yonge
Born Nantwich, Cheshire, 1868

Sue You
Born Saint Helena c.1862 (British subject aboard
Royal Navy ship *Flora*, Ascension, 1881 census)

—Z—

Canute Zane
Born St Thomas, Devon, 1870

Charles Zebedee Zebedee
Born Alderbury, Wiltshire, 1877

Thomas Zillion
Born Kippax, Yorkshire, c.1822 (Allerton Bywater, Yorkshire, 1851 census)

Maggie Zine
Born Kensington, London, c.1871 (Willesden, Middlesex, 1891 census)

Chapter Two

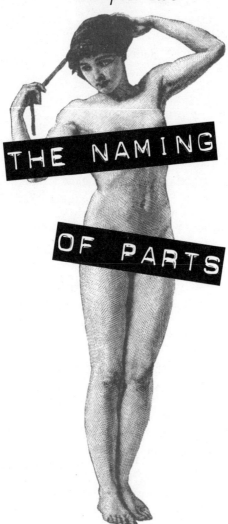

THE NAMING

OF PARTS

An Anatomy in Names

Fanny Barelegs
Born Hitchin, Hertfordshire, 1869

Betty Belly
Baptized Meigle, Perthshire, 10 November 1752

Charles Bigfoot
Married Eleanor Cummin, Aycliffe, Durham, 15 November 1767

Septuagesima Bone Bone
Born Walsingham, Norfolk, 1875

Betty Bowel
Baptized Dalton, Dumfries, 16 February 1764

Harry Liver Brain
Born Wortley, Yorkshire, 1877

Semen Brain
(Male) Born East Dean, Gloucestershire, c.1865 (East Dean, 1901 census)

Rosie Cheek
Born Grays, Essex, c.1897 (Grays, 1901 census)

Thirza Chuff
Born Totnes, Devon, 1837
*'Chuff' is one of those confusing slang words that, like 'Fanny',
can mean bottom or vagina.*

John Thomas Colon
Born Bradford, Yorkshire, 1876

Pierce Deare
Married Elizabeth Portman, St Gregory by Paul's, London, 14 April 1635

Rochmar Elbow
Married John Lyon, St Martin-in-the-Fields, London, 29 May 1809

Hyman Finger
Married Mile End, London, 1905

Rosina Knee Flower
Born Henley, Buckinghamshire, 1868

James Hoot Foot
Born Shaftesbury, Dorset, 1843

Phoebe Forehead
Baptized Shanklin, Isle of Wight, 6 April 1788

Tryphena Giblett
Born Easthampstead, Berkshire, 1859

Magdaline Gob
Married William Moncurr, Dundee, Angus, 22 June 1732

Bridget Groin
Died Bradford, Yorkshire, 1857

John Tummy Hague
Born Ecclesall Bierlow, Yorkshire, 1910

Orange Head
Born North Huish, Devon, c.1785
(Ugborough, Devon, 1861 census)

Dorothy Dimple H. Hermitage
Born Hastings, East Sussex, 1893

P. Hole
(Female) Married Wincanton, Somerset, 1842

Minnie Tongue Jags
Born Barton-upon-Irwell, Lancashire, 1886

Cornelius Kidney
Married Bodmin, Cornwall, 16 August 1820

I. Lash
(Male) Born Poplar, London, c.1890 (Wanstead, Essex, 1901 census)

Jemima Foot Legg
Born Dorchester, Dorset, 1841

Oliver Livers
Born Birmingham, Warwickshire, c.1891
(Aston, Warwickshire, 1901 census)

Patrick Mandible
Born Ireland c.1846 (Liverpool, 1881 census)

Amelia Mouth
Born Stepney, London, 1842

Amelia Muscle
Born Southampton, Hampshire, 1844

Naomi Nerve
Born Iden, Sussex, c.1824 (Playden, Kent, 1851 census)

Nellie Nose
Baptized St Mary Redcliffe, Bristol, Gloucestershire, 31 May 1877

Marie Ovary
Baptized Downton, Wiltshire, 4 April 1606

R. M. Pitt
(Female) Born Wolverhampton, Staffordshire, 1904

William Pulse
Died West Derby, Lancashire, 1880

Hannah Skeleton
Born Great Boughton, Cheshire, 1867

Esther Cowley Sperm
Born np c.1836; died Tynemouth, Northumberland, 1891

Joannes Mauritius Spleen
Baptized Gosport, Hampshire, 24 June 1789

Lymph Stanley
Born Croydon, Surrey, c.1881 (Ealing, Middlesex, 1901 census)

Caroline Stomach
Born Rotherham, Yorkshire, 1878

Lung Tack
Died West Derby, Lancashire, 1907

Jeani Talia
Born France c.1864 (St Andrew, Devon, 1891 census)

Bold Tongue
Married Bury, Lancashire, 1846

Sarah Tonin
Married Thomas Clark, St Dunstan, Stepney, London, 1813

Pearl Tooth
Born Steeples, Derbyshire, 1930

Betsey Wrinkle
Married Bolton, Lancashire, 1837

PLEASANT TITTY AND HER BOSOM CHUMS

◆

Sarah Baps
Married James Linsall, Debden, Essex, 16 October 1688

Rebecca Baretitt
Born Lincolnshire, c.1826 (Billingborough, Lincolnshire, 1841 census)

Fanny Boob
Born Manchester, Lancashire, c.1868 (Manchester, 1871 census)

Eliza Boobies
Married Tiverton, Devon, 1861
*Boobies is mainly a Devon name – a whole family of Boobies was
recorded in Poltimore at the time of the 1841 census.*

Triphena Bosom
Baptized St Mary the Virgin, Dover, Kent, nd July 1592

Jane Breast
Baptized St Matthew's, Douglas, Isle of Man, 4 February 1787

Seymour Bust
Born Halstead, Essex, 1841

Jemima Busty
Married Denis Boston, Hampton-in-Arden, Warwickshire, 25 November 1819

Myboob Bux
Born Kensington, London, 1859

Ellen Bristol Dancer
Born Stoke-on-Trent, Staffordshire, 1860

Jugs Ferner
Born Scotland c.1896 (East Ham, Essex, 1901 census)

Emma Hooters
Born London c.1839 (St Marylebone, London, 1851 census)
*Miss Hooters was recorded in the 1851 census as a twelve-year-old
nurse in the Baker Street home of bookseller and printer John G. Griffin.*

Fanny Knocker
Born np c.1829; died Dover, Kent, 1899

Lucy Mammary
Born Norfolk c.1844 (Southwark, London, 1891 census)

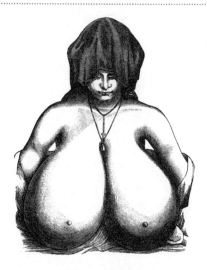

Melons Meakin
Married Basford, Nottinghamshire, 1897

Mary Melons
Married Thomas Jones, Talgarth, Breconshire, 19 February 1798

Elizabeth Nipple
Baptized St Mary Major, Exeter, Devon, 8 December 1772

Elizabeth Norks
Married Edward Nock, Aston, Warwickshire, 28 June 1758

Elsie Stitz
Born Chorlton, Lancashire, 1892

George Bunney Teat
Died Melton Mowbray, Leicestershire, 1839

Bosom Thaxter
(Male) Born Barningham, Norfolk, c.1811 (Gresham, Norfolk, 1851 census)

Tits Tillies
(Male) Born Rockingbourne, Hampshire, c.1878
(Fordingbridge, Hampshire, 1891 census)

Phebe Tit
Baptized Thundridge, Hertfordshire, 8 March 1790

Fanny Titball
Born Tetcott, Devon, c.1857 (Tetcott, 1871 census)

Willy Titcock
Born Bedfordshire c.1807 (Toddington, Bedfordshire, 1851 census)

Funny Titman
Born Rowell, Northamptonshire, c.1833
(Rowell, 1851 census)

Fanny Titsworth
Born Messingham, Lincolnshire, c.1856
(Gainsborough, Lincolnshire, 1891 census)

Charles Dud Titt
Born Wandsworth, London, 1909

Pleasant Titty
Baptized St John, Margate, Kent, 3 April 1768
*She was named after her mother, so there was a pair of
Pleasant Tittys in the family.*

Doris Topless
Born Sculcoates, Yorkshire, 1902

Ann Udder
Married Robert Andrew,
Buckland Monachorum, Devon,
5 September 1720

Allice [*sic*] Whoppers
Baptized St Nicholas, Gloucester,
22 December 1578

Juggy Williams
(Female) Married John Price, Almeley,
Herefordshire, 24 May 1792
and
Juggy Williams
(Male) Baptized Llywel, Breconshire,
25 July 1819

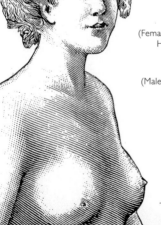

ANUS HORRIBILIS: THE BOTTOM LINE

———————◆———————

In his book The Compleat Practical Joker *(1953), American humorist H. Allen Smith relates:*

'In London, some years ago, a man named Pierce Bottom, weary of jokes about his name, spent several days combing through the telephone directories, seeking people who had "bottom" in their names. He found dozens – Bottom, Bottomley, Winterbottom, Throttlebottom, Greenbottom, Sidebottom, Higginbottom, and so on. He arranged for a dinner to be served in a sub-basement of a London building, and sent engraved invitations to all the "bottoms". Most of them showed up, but Pierce Bottom did not, and the guests found that each of them had to pay his own check. The entrée was rump roast.'

The story's authority is somewhat undermined by the fact that there is no evidence that anyone called 'Pierce Bottom' ever existed (not to mention 'Throttlebottom' and 'Greenbottom'), and in all probability it should be filed in the category of 'urban folktale'. The Oxford Dictionary of National Biography *credits the same tale to practical joker Horace De Vere Cole (1881–1936), as does the biography of his wife, Mavis. True or apocryphal? We leave you, the reader, to decide – but there's no denying 'bottom' names are pretty funny.*

Maria S. Aas
Born London c.1821 (Penge, Surrey, 1871 census)

Jemima Allass
Born np c.1861; died Barnsley, Yorkshire, 1893

Hephzibah Ann Anus
Born City of London 1850

Ursula Anus
Baptized Ponteland, Northumberland, 6 May 1610

Hugh Arse

Born Saint Mary Steps, Exeter, Devon, 1701

Arse was uncommon but not unknown as a surname in the 16th century: a John Arse (born c.1543) was recorded marrying a Marie Day in Rothley, Leicestershire, on 6 July 1568 – and how thrilled she must have been to find herself thenceforth known as 'Marie Arse'. From the 17th century we have a Dorothy Arse from Barnstaple, Devon, while in the 18th a whole family of Arses, probably of Spanish origin, resided in Milton Bryan, Bedfordshire, where Exequiel, son of Manuel Arse and Carmen Sagaseta, was baptized on 21 March 1877. His was the last Arse birth to be recorded, however, and by the time of the 1881 census, we find only an 'M. D. Arse', born in Germany in about 1855, a baker living in Holborn, London. The last of the British Arses had apparently all died of shame, changed their names, or perhaps emigrated to Bolivia, Mexico or Costa Rica where – numerically, at least – the Arses are much bigger.

Anus Arslanyan

Born 5 March 1917; died Bexley, Kent, 2004

Alexander Asole

Born North Shields,
Northumberland, c.1826
(Cornforth, Durham, 1851 census)

Caroline Ass

Born Kensington, London, 1849

Dick Assman

Born Birmingham, Warwickshire, c.1797
(Lambeth, London, 1851 census)

Arsabella Bending

Born Payhembury, Devon, c.1818
(Feniton, Devon, 1851 census)

Harquless George Bootyman

Died Hull, Yorkshire, 1899

Amelia Brown Bottom

Born Islington, London, 1876

Anice Bottom

Baptized Thornhill by Dewsbury,
Yorkshire, 14 May 1837

Arthur Henry Anulus Bottom
Baptized Sheffield, Yorkshire, 25 December 1859

Elizabeth Wildgoose Bottom
Baptized Bakewell, Derbyshire, 22 January 1826

Henry Goozee Bottom
Born Holborn, London, 1869

Huga Bottom
Born Nystad, Finland, c.1871 (Chief Mate of ship *Pallas*, Wallsend, Northumberland, 1901 census)

James Bottom Bottom Bottom*
Born Wakefield, Yorkshire, 1852

Joseph Liverpool Bottom
Born Great Boughton, Cheshire, 1842

Nora Bottom
Born Ecclesall Bierlow, Yorkshire, 1905

Original Bottom
Born Lockwood, Yorkshire, 1846

Popsie Bottom
(Female) Born Kent c.1891 (Kensington, London, 1891 census)

Silence Bottom
Married Thomas Mason, Chesterfield, Derbyshire, 26 October 1735

Sugden Green Bottom
Died Bradford, Yorkshire, 1855

Zippah Bottom
(Female) Born Whitley, Yorkshire, c.1832 (Thornhill, Yorkshire, 1901 census)

Huga Bottome
Baptized St Margaret's, Leicester, 10 March 1615

Total Bottomley
(Male) Born Manningham, Yorkshire, c.1858
(North Bierley, Yorkshire, 1861 census)

Truly Constant Bottomley
Born np c.1842; died Halifax, Yorkshire, 1907

*That's three Bottoms

James Seymour Bottoms
Born Ampthill, Bedfordshire, 1898

Frederick P. Botty
Born Islington c.1883 (Islington, 1901 census)

Botty Brown
(Female) Born Bolton, Lancashire, c.1790 (Bolton, 1851 census)

Willy Bum
Born Derbyshire, c.1836 (Glossop, Derbyshire, 1861 census)

Will Bumass
Born Birmingham, Warwickshire, c.1892
(Birmingham 1901 census)

Letitia Bumfastland
Born Holborn, London, c.1855 (Holborn, 1901 census)

Dick Bumfitt
Born Chorlton, Lancashire, 1898

Engelbert J. Bummer
Born Hull, Yorkshire, c.1847 (Holy Trinity, Yorkshire, 1871 census)

Fanny Bumpass
Born Brackley, Buckinghamshire, 1842

Annus Bumphrey
(Female) Born Broomhill, Northumberland, c.1860
(Ashington, Northumberland, 1891 census)

Christian Bums
Married London 19 February 1694

Isabella Bumup
Born Newcastle upon Tyne, Northumberland, c.1824
(Westgate, Northumberland, 1851 census)

Little Bunns
(Female) Born Spalding, Lincolnshire, c.1815
(Whittlesey, Cambridgeshire, 1871 census)

Annie Trollope Butt
Married Wandsworth, London, 1892

Bijou Butt
Born Okehampton, Devon, c.1860 (Gloucester, 1891 census)

Sarah Paine Butt
Married Stroud, Gloucestershire, 1891

Sexey Butt
Born Dundry, Somerset, c.1803 (Hanham, Gloucestershire, 1851 census)

Seymour Butt
Born Bath, Somerset, 1875

Sarah Buttholes
Born Finchley, London, c.1876 (Willesden, London, 1891 census)

Anthony Buttocks
Married Dorothy Thompson, Marske-by-the-Sea, Yorkshire, 24 January 1662

Susanah Ashworth Anus de Boothfould
Buried Newchurch in Rossendale, Lancashire, 11 April 1723

Maria Entry
Born Publow, Somerset, c.1813 (Bedminster, Somerset, 1861 census)

Fanny Fairbottom
Born Bridlington Quay, Yorkshire, c.1858 (Bridlington, 1861 census)

Sahara Arse Hayward
Born Bottseford, Wiltshire, c.1851
(St George Hanover Square, London, 1891 census)

William A. S. Hole
Born Burton upon Trent, Staffordshire, c.1887
(Buckhurst Hill, Essex, 1901 census)

Anus Hughes
Died St Asaph, Denbighshire, 1847

Annie Tush King
Born Shoreditch, London, c.1834 (Shoreditch, 1861 census)

Arundel Anus King
Born np c.1847; died Wellington, Somerset, 1904

Iva Longbottom
Born Balby, Yorkshire, c.1899 (Selby, Yorkshire, 1901 census)

Ann Nus
Married John Dixon, St Peter-at-Leeds, Leeds, Yorkshire, 4 February 1671

Alice Pinckass
Married Perranarworthal, Cornwall, 29 September 1711

Wonderful Ramsbottom
Born Dewsbury, Yorkshire, 1855

Nanny Rawbottom
Baptized Aston, Yorkshire, 5 April 1795

Joseph Man Rear
Baptized Heckington, Lincolnshire, 27 May 1820

Minnie Rosebottom
Born Ashton-under-Lyne, Lancashire, c.1888 (Ashton, 1901 census)

Benjamin Rump Rump
Born Aylsham, Norfolk, 1884

Lotta Rump
Born Flegg, Norfolk, 1902

Mary Sanus
Married Samuel Wilkinson, Birstall, Yorkshire, 29 July 1824

Mary Sarse
Born Holt, Worcestershire, c.1851 (Kempsey, Worcestershire, 1871 census)

Lincoln Entwistle Shipperbottom
Born Bolton, Lancashire, 1894
Almost all Shipperbottoms come from Bolton.

Obadiah Shoebottom
Baptized Rushton Spencer, Staffordshire, 26 March 1769

Eliza Shovebottom
Married Richard Allport, St Phillips, Birmingham, 3 October 1842

Benigna Shufflebottom
Died Haslingden, Lancashire, 1867

Asseley Sidebottom
Married William Shaw, Mottram-in-Longdendale, Cheshire, 3 September 1774

Sarah Smallass
Married John Watson, Tivetshall St Mary, Norfolk, 21 May 1751

Mary A. Stripperbottom
Born Bolton, Lancashire, c.1834 (Tonge with Haulge, Lancashire, 1891 census)

Arsley Swell
Baptized St Martin-in-the-Fields, London, 7 July 1745

Fanny Tush
Born Hull, Yorkshire, c.1849 (Sculcoates, Yorkshire, 1871 census)

Ann Whiteass
Baptized St Bridget, Chester, Cheshire, 21 March 1685

Arseman Whitteron
Born Plumpton, Yorkshire, c.1881 (Spofforth, Yorkshire, 1891 census)

Mary Windbottom
Born Salford, Lancashire, c.1855 (Salford, 1881 census)

Enema Bottomley Wood
Died Huddersfield, Yorkshire, 1904

◆

HAIR-RAISING NAMES

Rosalind Silver Beard
Born Edmonton, Middlesex, 1883

Storm Beard
Married Bath, Somerset, 1839

Wealthy Beard
Married Gloucester 1867

Betty Butterworth Beaver
Baptized St Michael, Ashton-under-Lyne, Lancashire, 8 January 1843

Harry Beaver
Baptized St Mary Portsea, Hampshire,
21 November 1812

Fanny Bevercomb
Born Wareham, Dorset, 1843

Curley Bush
(Male) Born Aldeburgh, Suffolk, c.1841 (Aldeburgh, 1851 census)

Fanny Bush
Married Francis Cox, Ringwood, Hampshire, 7 February 1824

Frances Rude Bush
Born West Ham, Essex, 1882

John Pecker Bush
Born Leeds, Yorkshire, 1883

Shave Copsey
Died Sudbury, Suffolk, 1852

Fanny Cutbush
Born Lewisham, London, 1839

Semen Fur
Born np 1913; died Bradford, Yorkshire, 2004

Rhoda Furbelow
Born Chippenham, Wiltshire, 1864

Annie Goatee
Married Droxford, Hampshire, 1880

Fanny Hair
Born Wallsall, Staffordshire, 1868

Pubecca Hare
Born Kent c.1831 (Minster, Kent, 1841 census)

Hairy Head
Born Dover, Kent, c.1878 (Dover 1891 census)

Merkin King
Born Nassington, Northamptonshire, c.1837 (Nassington, 1871 census)
A merkin is a pubic wig worn by prostitutes. The word first appeared in print in English in 1617.

Hairy Mann
Married Dover, Kent, 1894

Fanny Merkin
Born Thingoe, Suffolk, 1845

Hairy Percy Muckley
Born Kings Norton, Staffordshire, 1891

Archimedes Muff
Married Dewsbury, Yorkshire, 1848

Harry Muff
Born Bradford, Yorkshire, 1857

Catherine Pube
Married Thomas Jenkyn, Redruth, Cornwall, 1540

Susan J. Pubeblank
Born Bigbury, Devon, c.1862 (Bigbury, 1871 census)

Harry Pussey
Born Croydon, Surrey, c.1863 (Croydon, 1901 census)

Bald Scutt
Born Lancashire c.1840 (Middleton, Lancashire, 1841 census)

Jane Shaven Self
Born Clifton, Gloucestershire, 1841

Fanny Shaver
Married Stockton-on-Tees, Durham, 1842

Peter Twatt Shearer
Married Hampstead, London, 1900

William Dundreary Stevens
Born St George Hanover Square, London, 1862
Lord Dundreary is the bewhiskered character in Our American Cousin*, the play Abraham Lincoln was watching when he was assassinated in 1865; bushy sideburns became known as 'Dundrearys'.*

Mary Trimbush
Married Benjamin Ireland, St Mary, Portsea, Hampshire, 17 February 1806

Wiggy Watkin
Born Breconshire c.1786
(Aberystwyth, Monmouthshire, 1851 Wales census)

Ada Whisker Whisker
Born Walsingham, Norfolk, 1876

Fanny Wig
Born Hartley Wintney, Hampshire, 1838

Wilbart Charlesworth Wigfull Wigfull
Born Wortley, Yorkshire, 1846

◆

THE C-WORD

Perhaps surprisingly, despite its super-taboo status, 'cunt' and its variants crop up as both a first name and surname in Britain. It appeared within a number of British names in the medieval period: a Simon Sitbithecunte was recorded in Norfolk in 1167 in a Pipe Roll (a financial record), the boastfully named John Fillecunt was noted in a Lancashire Assize Roll of 1246, Robert Clevecunt in a Yorkshire Subsidy Roll of 1302 and Bele Wydecunthe in a Norfolk Subsidy Roll of 1328. Here are some more recent examples:

Mary Allcunt
Born Demerara, British Guiana, c.1815 (Chelsea, London, 1881 census)

Cunt Berger
Born Germany c.1878 (Sunderland, Durham, 1901 census)

Cuntin Churles
Born Yorkshire c.1861 (Chorlton-on-Medlock, Lancashire, 1891 census)

Cuntha Cronch
(Female) Born Middlesex c.1834 (St Marylebone, London, 1841 census)

A. Cunt
(Female) Baptized St James', Colchester, Essex, 1 March 1684

Fanny Cunt
Born Colchester, Essex, c.1839 (Hastings, East Sussex, 1891 census)
Fanny Cunt lived in the seaside resort of Hastings with a bunch of
Cunts: her son Richard (one hopes otherwise, but must assume he
was known as 'Dick Cunt') and her daughters Ella and Violet Cunt,
all of whom were born in Cape Colony (South Africa), and their
brother Alfred Cunt, born in New Zealand. Fanny is described as
'living on her own means' – presumably she had acquired her
unfortunate surname through marriage and returned from the
colonies with her four children, but apparently minus Mr Cunt.

Harry Cunt
Born Runcorn, Cheshire, c.1874
(mate of ship *Thistle*, Mersey, Lancashire, 1901 census)
As the captain claimed his name was Robert Ball, Harry (Hairy?) Cunt
may possibly have been a joke played on a naïve census enumerator.

Richard Harry Cunter
Born Romford, Essex, 1880

Worthy Cuntilla
Born Broughton, Wiltshire, c.1825 (Walcot, Somerset, 1861 census)

Lancelot S. Cuntin
Born Ely, Cambridgeshire, c.1899 (Ely, 1901 census)

Mary Cunting
Born Alverstoke, Hampshire, c.1837 (Portsea, Hampshire, 1861 census)

Joseph Cuntingdon
Born Portsea, Hampshire, c.1823 (Portsea, 1851 census)

Ellen Cuntly
Born Ireland c.1877 (Kensington, 1901 census)

James Cunts
Baptized Bank Street Unitarian Church, Bolton-le-Moors,
Lancashire, 28 May 1757

Margaret Cunty
Married John Hurley, St Anne, Soho, London 26 March 1798

Cunty Hoel
Born Warnham, Cheshire, c.1849
(Walton-on-the-Hill, Lancashire, 1871 census)
Cunty Hoel was the wife of Dick Hoel.

Mary Ann Cunt Hunt

Born Cheriton Fitzpaine, Devon, c.1829 (Thorverton, Devon, 1851 census)
Mary Ann and George F. Cunt Hunt were the parents of a girl baptized three months earlier with the same rhyming name as her mother.

Mike Hunt

Born Chippenham, Wiltshire, 1842

Temperance Kunt

(Female) Born Banwell, Somerset, c.1824 (Banwell, 1851 census)

Cunny Overend

(Female) Born Birkenhead, Cheshire, c.1870 (Birkenhead, 1871 census)
Cunny is a diminutive of cunt; it exists to this day as a rare surname, principally in the Manchester area.

Cunt Pepper

(Male) Born Smallthorne, Staffordshire, c.1828
(Burlsem, Staffordshire, 1851 census)

Emma Scunt

Born Harrow, Middlesex, c.1845 (Stepney, London, 1861 census)

Cuntliffe Fanny Vidal

Born Creeting St Mary, Suffolk, c.1887 (Creeting St Mary, 1891 census)

Kunt Zonar

Born Scotland c.1828 (Gorbals, Lanarkshire, 1841 Scotland census)

◆

THE UPS AND DOWNS OF 'FANNY'

Eagle-eyed readers will note the prevalence of 'Fanny' names throughout. This is as much a reflection of its popularity as of its double entendre *potential. 'Fanny' gradually replaced Frances as a baptismal name, rather than a nickname, from the second half of the eighteenth century, John Cleland's popular novel,* Fanny Hill: Memoirs of a Woman of Pleasure, *dating from 1748, perhaps contributing to its success. It peaked in the 1870s, when more than 5,000 girls were given the name every year, but then began a steady decline which perhaps reflected the rise in the use of 'fanny' as a slang word for the female gen-*

itals. Its earliest recorded use in print appeared in the September 1879 issue of the salacious magazine The Pearl, *with the phrase, 'You shan't look at my fanny for nothing' – quite so. Thereafter, it became progressively less common, so that by the time it featured in songs and ribald jokes in the trenches of the First World War, it had all but fallen out of use. By the Second World War, scarcely anyone was given the name 'Fanny'. The 1944 British film* Fanny by Gaslight, *based on the novel of that name by Michael Sadleir, received such an outraged reaction that in the US it was retitled* Man of Evil *– even though it did not mean quite the same thing. The American use of 'fanny' for the bottom dates from the 1920s, the differing meaning resulting in occasional confusion. (On the author's first visit to the USA in the early 1970s, he was astonished when a woman told him that she preferred not to wear jeans because, she claimed, she had 'an enormous fanny'.) Here is just a sampling of the Fannies of yesteryear:*

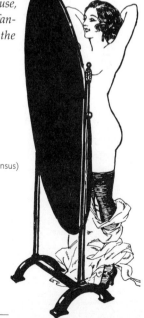

Fanny Affection
Born np c.1815
(Watford, Hertfordshire, 1871 census)

Fanny Box
Born Chippenham, Wiltshire, 1839

Fanny B. Bythesea
Born India c.1847 (Bath, Somerset, 1881 census)

Loveday Fanny Cocks
Born Liskeard, Cornwall, 1849

Fanny Coil
Born Chester, Cheshire, 1898

Fanny Crease
Born Reading, Berkshire, c.1878
(Reading, 1901 census)

Fanny Crotch
Baptized St Martin at Palace, Norwich, Norfolk, 13 July 1624

Fanny Bollock Cullis
Married Islington, London, 1856

Fanny Dogger
Born Norton, Hertfordshire, c.1859 (Norton, 1871 census)

Fanny Eighteen
Born Great Glemham, Suffolk, c.1863 (Reading, Berkshire, 1901 census)

Fanny Fanny
Baptized St Pancras, Middlesex, 1837

Quadruna Fanny Fewster
Born Stockton-on-Tees, Durham, 1893

Fanny Fidget
Died Portsea, Hampshire, 1868

Fanny Flick
Born Clerkenwell, London, 1842

Fanny Flow
Born Newport, Isle of Wight, c.1844 (Chelsea, London, 1901 census)

Fanny Funk
Born Whitechapel, London, 1859

Fanny Funt
Born St Leonard, Shoreditch, London, c.1853 (St Leonard, 1881 census)
As was said of the surname of Allen Funt (1914–99),
the creator of the TV show Candid Camera, *'Funt' is neither*
one thing or another.

Fanny Gash
Baptized Syston, Lincolnshire, 29 July 1838

Fortunate Fanny Hinder
Born Cirencester, Gloucestershire, 1884

Fannys [*sic*] Hole
Born Farnham, Surrey, c.1867 (Westminster, London, 1891 census)

Fanny Honey
Buried Padstow, Cornwall, 12 November 1891

Fanny Humpage
Born Dudley, Staffordshire, 1876

Fanny Ing
Born Thame, Oxfordshire, 1854

Fanny Lather
Married Tonbridge, Kent, 1873

Fanny Lingo
Born Bedford 1852

Fanny Lips
Married John Christophers, Falmouth, Cornwall, 13 April 1823

Fanny Lover
Married Marylebone, London, 1850

Fanny Lust
Born Lewes, Sussex, 1844

Fanny Alotta Mould
Born np c.1858; died Newmarket, Suffolk, 1868

Fanny Organ
Born Frome, Somerset, 1838

Fanny Jane Penis
Born Gloucester 1842

Fanny Plenty
Born Shoreditch, London, 1867

Fanny Pounder
Born Manchester, Lancashire, 1879

Fanny Pussephette
Born Hertfordshire c.1833
(Flamstead, Hertfordshire, 1841 census)

Fanny Pussey
Born Yorkshire c.1817 (Holderness, Yorkshire, 1841 census)

Nine Fanny Rogers
Married Whitchurch, Shropshire, 1905

Many Fanny Salisbury
Born Wrexham, Denbighshire, 1898

Fanny Pink Simons
Married Spilby, Lincolnshire, 1859

Fanny Spong
Born Woking, Surrey, 13 March 1858

Pubete Fanny Steel
Born Morley, Yorkshire, c.1887 (Morley, 1901 census)

Fanny Strain
Born Dudley, Staffordshire, 1867

Fanny Tingle
Born Worsley, Lancashire, 1848

Fanny Warmer
Married Newent, Gloucestershire, 1875

Fanny Warning
Born Northamptonshire c.1862 (Kensington, London, 1881 census)

Fanny Washer
Married Axbridge, Somerset, 1846

Fanny Wonder
Married Whitechapel, London, 1907

See also: The Names of the Game, Reverse Names and throughout for yet more Fannies.

───◆───

MORE LADIES' PARTS

Clit Beatley
Born Carlton, Lincolnshire, c.1797
(Grainthorpe, Lincolnshire, 1871 census)

Yoni Boland
Born Epping, Essex, 1911
*'Yoni' is Sanskrit for 'divine passage',
but is often misinterpreted
as meaning 'vagina'.*

Vegina Mode Bradley
Born Bishop Auckland, Durham, 1876

Charlotte Crotch
Born Norwich, Norfolk, 1846

Elizabeth Flaps
Baptized St Andrew Holborn, London, 31 March 1695

Labia Hood
Born Nottingham c.1843 (Snelland, Nottinghamshire, 1861 census)

M. Inge
(Female) Born Eastry, Kent, 1840

Minkie Miles
Born Hammersmith, London, c.1895 (Fulham, London, 1901 census)

Harry Minge
Born West Derby, Lancashire, 1911

Caroline Minky
Baptized St Dunstan, Stepney, London, 14 November 1860

Vagina Prior
Born Chelsea, London, nd (Chelsea, 1881 census)

Seymour Pussy
Baptized St Laurence, Catsfield, Sussex, 18 June 1836

Mary Quim
Baptized Dartford, Kent, 11 March 1770

Pudendiana Ryan
(Female) Born Viracapatam, India, nd (Bury, Lancashire, 1891 census)

Eliza Scrack
Born Cuckfield, Sussex, 1873

Lucy Snatch
Married Robert Colley, St Dunstan, Stepney, London, 11 June 1644

Euphemia Twat
Baptized Walls, Shetland, 1800

There were forty-eight Twats in Orkney and Shetland at the time of the 1841 census. In this same year, in his poem Pippa Passes*, Robert Browning included the line 'Cowls and twats', later explaining to the editor of the* Oxford English Dictionary *that he thought a 'twat' was a kind of hood worn by nuns. He was wrong.*

Jamima Twat
Born Tingwall, Shetland, 12 November 1833

Philadelphia Twat
Baptized Walls, Shetland, 1793

Emelie Vegina
Born Longeuil, Canada, c.1848 (Golcar, Yorkshire, 1881 census)

◆

COCK-EYED NAMES: CLEVER DICKS, PRICKS AND WILLIES

John Thomas Badcock
Baptized Great Bowden, Leicestershire, 18 June 1868

Mildred Rose Baldcock
Born Holborn, London, c.1862 ('prostitute', Paddington, London, 1881 census)
There was little euphemism or political correctness in Victorian census returns: individuals were routinely described as 'prostitute', 'brothel keeper' or 'criminal', or even 'idiot', 'imbecile' or 'lunatic'.

Dick Barecock
Baptized Stagsden, Bedfordshire, 29 August 1790

Betsy Cockin Beevers
Died Huddersfield, Yorkshire, 1852

Dick Bellend
Baptized St Mary Magdalene, Bermondsey, London, 6 February 1848

Willy Bicardick
Baptized Franham, Yorkshire, 10 July 1576

Jane Cock Burgers
Born Camborne, Cornwall, c.1817 (Camborne, 1861 census)

Fanny Cleaver
Baptized St Michael, Coventry 8 June 1755
A 'fanny cleaver' is a slang term for a large penis.

Alice Ada Cock
Born Wapping, London, c.1846 (Covent Garden, London, 1871 census)

Dick Cock
Born Saffron Walden, Essex, 1852

Epiphany Bullock Cock
Born St Austell, Cornwall, 1844

Everard Cock
Born Wells, Somerset, 1890

Faithful Cock
Married St Columb Major, Cornwall, 1 January 1708

George Alfred Pink Cock
Born Shoreditch, London, 1852

Hugh Cock
Married Charlotte Over, Mevagissey, Cornwall, 19 June 1825

John Thomas Cock
Born np c.1859; died Penzance, Cornwall, 1894
*One of at least sixteen John Thomas Cocks born in
the period 1837–1906.*

Lovely Cock
(Female) Born Cornwall c.1781 (Mylor, Cornwall, 1841 census)

William Curling Cock
Born Dover, Kent, 1861

Rose Cockhead
Born Bladon, Oxfordshire, c.1874 (Begbroke, Oxfordshire, 1901 census)

Champagne Cocks
Born Medhurst, Kent, April 1906

Frederick Seymour Cocks
Born Darlington, Durham, 1882
*Labour MP for Broxtowe, Nottinghamshire, 1924–54,
known as Seymour Cocks.*

Henry Lovedy Cox Cocks
Born Gloucestershire c.1821 (Hackney, London, 1871 census)

Ophelia Cocks
Born Oxfordshire c.1800 (St Marylebone, London, 1871 census)

Ernest Dick
Born Sunderland, Durham, 1881

Little Dick
Born Northroad, Cheshire, c.1851 (Wolstanton, Staffordshire, 1881 census)

Thomas Hardy Dick
Born Sculcoates, Yorkshire, 1883

William Hardy Dick
Born Sculcoates, Yorkshire, 1883

*With Thomas Hardy Dick above, there were two Hardy Dicks
born in the same town in the same year.*

Ann Dickcock
Married Roger Willis, St James', Southbroom, Devizes, Wiltshire,
1 October 1738

Willie Manhood Dickerson
Born King's Lynn, Norfolk, 1864

Odd Dicks
Died Thrapston, Northamptonshire, 1886

Harry Dong
Born Birmingham, Warwickshire, c.1847
(Edgbaston, Warwickshire, 1861 census)

John Thomas Dong
Born Bradford, Yorkshire, c.1868 (Bradford, 1901 census)

Willy Donger
Born Barnstaple, Devon, 1855

Dick End
Married Sarah Hunt, Lacock, Wiltshire, 21 July 1755

P. Enis
(Male) Born Lancashire c.1806 (Manchester, Lancashire, 1841 census)

Dick Everhard
Married Frances Lee, Billesley, Warwickshire, 11 September 1653

Harry Goldcock
Born Hackington, Kent, c.1891 (Canterbury, Kent, 1891 census)

Prick Green
(Male) Born Preston, Lancashire, c.1863 (Clitheroe, Lancashire, 1881 census)

Helmet North Guest
Born Hull, Yorkshire, 1889

Mealota Hardcock
Born Norfolk c.1832 (Spotland, Lancashire, 1861 census)

Catharine Harddick
Baptized Ollerton, Nottinghamshire, 7 June 1725

John Knobs Henry
Born Cookstown, Ireland, c.1837 (Greenwich, Kent, 1881 census)

Love Hiscock
Baptized Mere, Wiltshire, 18 April 1825

Mike Hock
Born Wigan, Lancashire, 1892

Charles Penis Horn
Married St George Hanover Square, London, 1845

Prick Hucklesbury
Born Framlingham, Suffolk, c.1811 (Woodbridge, Suffolk, 1871 census)

William Dick Inches
Born Alyth, Perth, 25 August 1830

Dick Knob
Married Elizabeth Flower, Beeston, Nottinghamshire, 14 November 1682

Nathaniel Knob
Born Bristol, Somerset, c.1868 (Battersea, London, 1891 census)

Henri Le Dong
Married Amy L. Williams, Swansea, Glamorgan, 1915

Dick Less
Born Stepney, London, c.1861 (Limehouse, 1891 census)

Letitia P. Lingam
Born Cosgrove, Northamptonshire, c.1858
(Birkenhead, Cheshire, 1901 census)
The lingam is the male counterpart of the yoni –
see Yoni Boland, above.

Willy Long
(Female) Born Luton, Bedfordshire, c.1896 (Luton, 1901 census)

Willy Longcock
Born np 1833 (Lambeth, London, 1861 census)

George Longdong
Born Frodingham, Yorkshire, c.1858 (Frodingham, 1861 census)

Elizabeth Lovescock
Baptized St Giles without Cripplegate, London, 21 February 1727

Fred Knoblock Lowcock
Married Keighley, Yorkshire, 1890

Dick Manhood
Baptized Glemsford, Suffolk, 17 May 1657

Wanger Rhoda Mantropp
(Female) Born Lowestoft, Suffolk, c.1874 (Swaffham, Norfolk, 1901 census)

Jemima Merrycock
Married Joseph Scott, St Margaret's, King's Lynn, Norfolk, 6 September 1829

Mary Ann Morecock Morecock
Born Wokingham, Berkshire, 1842

Harriet Nicewonger
Born Ilkeston, Derbyshire, c.1876 (Ilkeston, 1891 census)

P. Nile
(Male) Born St Austell, Cornwall, 1897

Juan P. Nis
Baptized Blanchland, Northumberland, 30 April 1837

William Nocock
Born Surrey c.1837 (Oxted, Surrey, 1841 census)

John Thomas Organ
Born Newport, Monmouthshire, 1856

Chris Peacock
Born Askrigg, Yorkshire, 1837

Claude Pecker
Born Atcham, Shropshire, 1897

Thomas Penis
Baptized Kendal, Westmorland, 22 December 1717

Fanny Penix
Born Elsecar, Yorkshire, c.1889 (Elsecar, 1901 census)

Marianne Penus
Married John Claudius Bitton, St Botolph, London, 29 February 1736

John Penusardon
Born Pancrasweek, Devon, c.1814 (Pancrasweek, 1851 census)

Harry Chopper J. Percy
Born Gravesend, Kent, 1879

Dick Prick
Born np c.1790; died Machynlleth, Powys, 1870

Hugh Prick
Born Shropshire c.1801 (Oswestry, Shropshire, 1851 census)

Misericordia Prick
Married Susanna Land, Stansfield, Suffolk, 4 July 1731

Curly Dick Radcliffe
Born Swansea, Glamorgan, 1904

P. Rick
(Male) Married Ann Gouding, St Dunstan, Stepney, London, 29 March 1835

Mike Rotch
Born Ireland c.1817 (Stockport, Cheshire, 1861 census)

Penis Rough
Born Ireland c.1831 (Liverpool, Lancashire, 1871 census)

Elizabeth Scock
Married Phillip Postle, Great Yarmouth, Norfolk, 29 September 1745

George Silvercock
Born Bethnal Green, London, c.1857 (Bethnal Green, 1881 census)

Oliver Slowcock
Baptized St Mary Whitechapel, Stepney, London, May 1778

Dick Smallpiece
Baptized Cranley, Surrey, 6 October 1793

John Willie Soft
Born Macclesfield, Cheshire, 1893

Gladys Treblecock Stanton
Died Neath, Glamorgan, 1908

Dick Surprise
Born Cheshire c.1822 (Chester, Cheshire, 1851 census)

John Todger
Born Gringham, Dorset, c.1825 (Weston-super-Mare, Somerset, 1891 census)

Hugh Tool
Born Cumberland c.1850 (Wolsingham, Durham, 1881 census)

John Thomas Tool
Born Weardale, Durham, 1873

John Long Toole
Born Stonehouse, Devon, c.1842 (Devonport, Devon, 1871 census)

Willy Treblecock
Born St Marylebone, London, 1850

John Shaw Twilley
Born Helmsley, Yorkshire, 1873

James Twococks
Born Bermondsey, London, 1861

Hugh Wang
Baptized St Oswald, Durham, 14 February 1568

Minnie Wanger
Born Stepney, London, 1872

Willie Warmer
Born Mitford, Norfolk, 1883

Dick Whatcock
Married Sarah Fletcher, Edgbaston, Warwickshire, 27 February 1731

Any Willie
Born Pembroke 1862

Hugh Willy
Baptized Old Kilpatrick, Dunbarton, 3 November 1743

John Thomas Willy
Baptized St George the Martyr, Southwark, London, 25 December 1812

Willy Willy
Born Ireland c.1844 (Kensington, London, 1851 census)

Zippora Willy
Baptized Warmington, Warwickshire, 23 December 1785

Dick Willyman
Married Jennet Smythe, Snaith, Yorkshire, 12 February 1597

Dick Wiper
Born np 1913; died Dewsbury, Yorkshire, 1998

A LOAD OF BALLS

Abraham Ball
Born Greasley, Nottinghamshire, c.1811
('castrator', Greasley, 1881 census)

Ball Ball
Born Tisbury, Wiltshire, 1890

Ellis Poo Ball
Born Leeds, Yorkshire, 1842

Ophelia Ball
Born Ashby-de-la-Zouch, Leicestershire, 1874

William Loose Ball
Married Holsworthy, Cornwall, 1888

Comfort Balls
Married Mitford, Norfolk, 1879

Golden Balls
Baptized Aylsham, Norfolk, 26 September 1813
His son was also called Golden Balls.

Happy Balls
Born Blything, Suffolk, 1878

Harry Balls
Married Thingoe, Suffolk, 1869

Horatio Finer Balls Balls
Born St Luke, London, 1842

Minnie Balls
Born West Ham, Essex, 1870

Norah Balls
Born North Shields, Northumberland, c.1887
(Tynemouth, Northumberland, 1901 census)

Myball Barton
Born Lancashire c.1816 (Preston, Lancashire, 1841 census)

Dick Bollock
Married Dorathy [*sic*] Marten, St Mabyn, Cornwall, 16 June 1659

William Bollocks
Married Anne Hodges, Withington, Herefordshire, 13 November 1574

Arnold Eunuch
Married Ann Mabie, Sherburn-in-Elmet, Yorkshire, 25 January 1701

Balls Garrett
Born Leiston, Suffolk, 11 May 1810

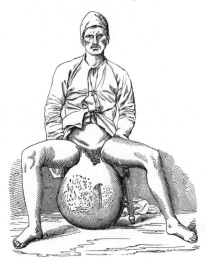

William Gonad
Baptized Fyfield, Wiltshire, 7 August 1774

Mahala Honeyballs
Baptized Fordham, Essex, 10 March 1811

Sidney Herbert Knacker
Baptized St Mary the Virgin, Dover, Kent, 13 January 1803

Ann Bollock Lovelace
Married Dorchester, Dorset, 1861

John Nadger
Married Elizabeth Lund, Plumpton, Lancashire, 31 January 1704

Chapter Three

THE NAMES
OF THE GAME

ON THE JOB

Sarah Amorous
Married Jonathan Everit, Wheathampstead, Hertfordshire, 1 August 1780

Isabella Anal
Married David Moneypenny, St Andrews and St Leonards, Fife,
4 December 1835

Charlotte Anally
Baptized St John Portsea, Hampshire, 24 January 1813

Alice Banger Banger
Born Bridport, Dorset, 1888

Fanny Dicks Beebe
Born Thrapston, Huntingdonshire, 1860

Eliza Bondage
Baptized St George the Martyr, Southwark, London, 1 March 1812

Daily Boner
(Female) Born Hernhill, Kent, c.1898 (Hernhill, 1901 census)

Emma Hedwig M. Bonk
Married Westminster, London, 1888

Anne Pretty Johns Bonker
Married Kingsbridge, Devon, 1842

Lizzie Bonking
Born Hannington, Surrey, c.1878 (Clerkenwell, London, 1891 census)

Rebecca Bonks
Baptized St Pancras, London, 17 November 1839

Rogers Boys
Born Newport, Monmouthshire, c.1848 (Newton Abbot, Devon, 1901 census)

Dorothy Brothel
Married Henry Shipp, Wigtoft, Lincolnshire, 21 March 1705

Erasmus Bugger
Born North Shields, Northumberland, c.1876 (Hackney, London, 1901 census)

Mary Buggery
Born Stourbridge, Worcestershire, 1852

Fanny Buster
Born St Albans, Hertfordshire, c.1866 (St Albans, 1891 census)

Fanny Carnal
Baptized Feniton, Devon, 24 June 1733

Fanny Cathouse
Born Darnham, Wiltshire, c.1868 (Alfreton, Derbyshire, 1881 census)

Fanny Chaffer
Born Westhampnett, Sussex, 1864

John Benjamin Fister Christian
Born Eastry, Kent, 1859

William Deviant Christie
Born Hackney, London, 1845

Rhoda Cock
Married Thomas Lovack, South Lopham, Norfolk, 9 February 1815

Ellen Fanny Cockaday
Born Norwich, Norfolk, 23 June 1880

Percy Cockfit
Born Chelmsford, Essex, 1867

Mary Cockfull
Died Huddersfield, Yorkshire, 1852

Ulaya Cockin
Baptized St Agnes, Cornwall, 9 December 1673

Anne Cocklove
Married Richard Taylor, St Gregory by Paul's, London, 23 February 1608

Dick Cockout
Baptized Manchester Cathedral, Manchester, Lancashire, 17 May 1796

Fanny Cockup
Born Dartford, Kent, 1840

Jane Coldtart
Married West Derby, Lancashire, 1857

Dick Comes
Born Thorpe, Surrey, c.1798 (Thorpe, 1851 census)
Dick Comes was the father of Willy Comes.

Fanny Comes
Baptized Witton-cum-Twambrooks, Cheshire, 25 October 1857

Dick Condom
Born St Marylebone, Middlesex, c.1845 (St Marylebone, 1851 census)

Fanny Congress
Born Spalding, Lincolnshire, c.1819 (Spalding, 1891 census)

Fanny Creamer
Born Pocklington, Yorkshire, 1872

Susanna Cum
Married Thomas Louch, Ottery St Mary, Devon, 11 June 1806

Isabella Deviant
Born np c.1806 (Portsea, Hampshire, 1841 census)

Henry Cock Dicker
Born np c.1822; died Plymouth, Devon, 1880

Susan Harde Dicker
Born Brixton, Devon, c.1855 (Totnes, Devon, 1871 census)

John Large Dickin
Married Wem, Shropshire, 1870

Fanny Dicking
Baptized Helion Bumpstead, Essex, 17 February 1721

Fanny Dickwell
Born Butterwick, Lincolnshire, c.1859 (Leake, Lincolnshire, 1861 census)
*Fanny was the daughter of Willy Dickwell Snr and
sister of Willy Dickwell Jnr.*

Jenet Dildo
Married William Withington, Eccles, Lancashire, 1614

Bridget Dogging
Born Ireland c.1869 (Barony, Lanarkshire, 1891 census)
*The etymology of the British slang term 'dogging' – engaging in sex in
public places – has not yet been definitively established, but one
school of thought claims it derives from the common response of men
caught in search of such activities, as participant or voyeur, 'I was
just walking the dog…'*

Willy Droop
Born Steinhagen, Germany, c.1866 (Camberwell, London, 1891 census)

Harlot Duncan
Married Glanford Brigg, Lincolnshire, 1867

S. Emen
(Female) Born Brill, Buckinghamshire, c.1790
(Tring, Hertfordshire, 1851 census)

Horny Ende
Born Warwickshire c.1830 (Birmingham, Warwickshire, 1841 census)

Emma Erecter
Born np c.1863 (Sheffield, Yorkshire, 1901 census)

Rhoda Fanny
Born Widnes, Lancashire, c.1876 (Eccleston, Lancashire, 1891 census)

Fanny Feeling
Born Hampshire c.1801 (Northwood, Hampshire, 1841 census)

Frank Felch
Died Bedford 1869
*Felching is a sexual practice too rude to explain in a
family book such as this.*

Fanny Felcher
Born Pattinghager, Staffordshire, c.1874 (Worfield, Shropshire, 1851 census)

Charlotte Fillass
Born Shoreditch, London, 1860

Fanny Filling
Born Horsham, Sussex, c.1832 (Lingfield, Surrey, 1901 census)

Fanny Finger
Born Ide Hill, Kent, c.1859 (Blacklands, Sussex, 1891 census)

Fanny Fister
Born Weymouth c.1859 (Parkstone, Dorset, 1891 census)

Mary Y. Fisting
Born Essex c.1839 (Radipole, Dorset, 1871 census)

Thomas Flasher
Married Mary Barrett, Nethley, Yorkshire, 15 April 1786

Ebenezer Flirt
Born Middlesex c.1865 (St Pancras, London, 1881 census)

Freelove Flower
Born Bath, Somerset, 1849

John Carnal Fox
Married Stoke-on-Trent, Staffordshire, 1851

Lucy Ada Frig
Baptized Stowe Nine Churches, Northamptonshire, 10 September 1874

Fanny Frigger
Died Beckley, Northiam, Sussex, 17 March 1849

Robert Goldspunk
Born Middlesex c.1837 (Bethnal Green, London, 1841 census)

Christiana Gush Good
Born Stoke Damerel, Devon, 1865

Mary Goodlay
Married George Brown, Rougham, Suffolk, 19 November 1741

Cum E. Gook
(Female) Born London c.1833
(St George Hanover Square, London, 1851 census)

N. Gorge
(Female) Born Norfolk c.1840 (Larling, Norfolk, 1841 census)

L. E. Gover
(Female) Born South Stoneham,
Hampshire, 1894

Sibella Grope
Baptized Manaccan,
Cornwall, 28 December 1829

Harris Groper
Born St George in the East, London, 1902

Fanny Growcock
Born Bourne, Lincolnshire, 1852

Randy Guest
Born Sussex c.1795
(Wadhurst, Sussex, 1841 census)

Martha Gusher
Born Pershore, Worcestershire, c.1858
(Pershore, 1871 census)

Dorothy Needs Guy
Born Penzance, Cornwall, 1899

S. Hag
Married Henry Beerlin, St Mary the Virgin, Dover, Kent, 2 January 1800

S. Hagger
(Female) Baptized Great Chishall, Essex, 7 May 1646

Dick Hardon
Buried Auckland, Durham, 25 April 1571

Ivor Hardon
Born Llansamlet, Glamorgan, c.1878 (Swansea, Glamorgan, 1891 Wales census)

Penis Hardon
(Male) Born Ireland c.1811 (Fulham, London, 1851 census)

Dorcas Harlot
Died Northampton 1879

Ophelia Fanny Hole
Born Bristol, Gloucestershire, 1859

Phyllis Hole
Born Greenwich, London, 1906

Phyllis Private Holes
Born Eastbourne, East Sussex, 1893

Seraphim Hooker
(Male) Born Exeter, Devon, c.1796 (Exeter, 1851 census)

Roger Horny
Baptized Lindridge, Worcestershire, 1628

Fanny Humper
Born Clerkenwell, London, c.1842
(St Luke, Old Street, London, 1851 census)

Martha Incest
Born Whitechapel, London, c.1899 (West Ham, Essex, 1901 census)

Dick Ing
Baptized Long Crendon, Buckinghamshire, 1 February 1858

Lothario Othello Ingham
Born Sculcoates, Yorkshire, 1880

Raper Jagger
Born Leeds, Yorkshire, 1842

Carnal Jarvis
Born Wisbech, Cambridgeshire, 1852

Mary Jezebel
Baptized Loversall, Yorkshire, 6 June 1756

Fanny Jiggles
Born Ampthill, Bedfordshire, 1859

Fanny Juice
Baptized St Margaret, Westminster, London, 12 March 1650

Dick Justin
Baptized St Andrew, Holborn, London, 4 October 1685

Hardon King
Born np c.1828 (St James, Clerkenwell Green, London, 1841 census)

Fanny Kiss
Died Epping, Essex, 1874

Phil Lander
Born Stoke Damerel, Devon, 1846

Analey Larking
Died Sevenoaks, Kent, 1843

E. C. Lay
(Female) Born Lizard, Cornwall, c.1862
(Pendeen, Cornwall, 1871 census)

Francis Pervert Leconte
Born Holborn, London, 1887

Mo Lester
(Male) Born Wigan, Lancashire, 1875

Kerenhappuch Letch
Married Elijah Davey, Great Yarmouth, Norfolk, 30 July 1827

Clementina Labia Lever
Born Nottingham 1897

Priscilla Lewd
Born Lincolnshire c.1806 (Boston, Lincolnshire, 1841 census)

Ogshort Boner Lewis
(Male) Born Holyhead, Anglesey, c.1865 (Holyhead, 1881 census)

James Higginson Lovebody
Baptized St Peter's, Liverpool, 1 September 1830

Alberta Lovetoy
Born Windsor, Berkshire, c.1879 (Plumstead, London, 1891 census)

Lucy Lube
Born Preston, Lancashire, c.1830 (Formby, Lancashire, 1881 census)

John Bonker Luscombe
Born np c.1816; died Plympton St Mary, Cornwall, 1897

Jet Lust
Born Oxfordshire c.1840 (Drayton, Oxfordshire, 1841 census)

Herbert Lusty Lusty
Born Stroud, Gloucestershire, 1902

Thomas Fondle Manning
Married Yarmouth, Norfolk, 1848

James McAnal
Born Ireland c.1801 (Liverpool, Lancashire, 1841 census)

Roger Mee
Died Bolton, Lancashire, 1856

Thomas Molester
Born Middlesex c.1834 (Hackney, London, 1841 census)

Comes More
Born Middlesex c.1821 (Covent Garden, London, 1841 census)

Dick Myass
Baptized Hornsea, Yorkshire, 26 January 1804

Roger Mycock
Born np 1913; died King's Lynn, Norfolk, 1997

Fanny Nookey
Baptized Ashcott, Somerset, 28 July 1872

Nicholas Orgy
Baptized St Martin-in-the-Fields, London, 26 December 1626

Elizabeth Spunk Oxley
Born Dewsbury, Yorkshire, 1871

Humping M. C. Palmer
(Male) Born Newbury, Berkshire, c.1872 (Newbury, 1881 census)

Nancy Passion
Born St George in the East, London, 1904

Elizabeth Sex Pechey
Born Docking, Norfolk, 1846

Vincent Pedo
Married Sophia Weatherwise, St Leonard, Shoreditch,
London, 5 February 1827

George Spurt Percival
Born Camberwell, London, 1852

Trannie Pickup
(Female) Born Portsmouth, Hampshire, c.1853 (Grays, Essex, 1901 census)

George Pimp
Born Sleaford, Lincolnshire, 1860

Alice May Poke
Born Sheffield, Yorkshire, 1896

Fanny Poker
Born Henley-on-Thames, Oxfordshire, c.1877
(Remenham, Berkshire, 1901 census)

Fanny Porn
Born Nutley, Hampshire, c.1849 (Nutley, 1861 census)

Porndance Powell
(Female) Born Blackwell, Worcestershire, c.1841
(Sedgley, Staffordshire, 1871 census)

Harlot Price
(Male) Born Shropshire c.1832 (Clun, Shropshire, 1841 census)

Ada Prick
Born np c.1878; died Sheffield 1907

Simon Prickadvance
Married Mary Lullham, Peasmarsh, Sussex, 8 May 1682

Fanny Pricklove
Born Waltham Abbey, Essex (Sewardstone, Essex, 1851 census)

Mary Anne Prickup
Born Newton Moor, Cheshire, c.1827 (Dukinfield, Lancashire, 1861 census)

Ray Pugh
Born Ashton-under-Lyne, Lancashire, 1898

Dick Pumper
Born Clee Hills, Shropshire, c.1826 (Kingswinford, Staffordshire, 1851 census)

Fanny Pumper
Born Mile End, London, c.1879 (St George in the East, London, 1881 census)

Amoral Bessie Purchase
Born Langport, Somerset, 1891

Roger Quicklove
Baptized St Mary, Whittlesey, Cambridgeshire, 11 June 1629

Mary Rampant
Baptized Dorking, Surrey, 21 February 1713

Raper Raper
Born Bridlington, Yorkshire, 1843

Large Mounting Ratcliffe
Born Haslingden, Lancashire, c.1885 (Haslingden, 1901 census)

Richard Ravish
Baptized St Mildred Poultry without St Mary Colechurch,
London, 6 September 1685

Dick Rider
Born Hungerford, Berkshire, 1839

William Horny Robinson
Born Hull, Yorkshire, c.1847 (Hull, 1901 census)

G. Roper
(Male) Baptized St Margaret, Westminster, London, 22 May 1552

Loveday Rutter
Buried Wendron, Cornwall, 16 February 1783

Willie Rutting
Born London c.1882 (Chertsey, Surrey, 1891 census)

Come Saladin
Died Southampton, Hampshire, 1888

Annie Scandal
Born Leeds, Yorkshire, c.1883 (Hunslet, Yorkshire, 1891 census)

Shafter Scorer
(Male) Born Hetton-le-Hole, Durham, c.1866
(Broom, Durham, 1901 census)

Mary Screws
Married Edward Taylor, Canterbury, Kent, 2 January 1710

Sod Self
(Male) Born Bromley, Kent, c.1899 (Bromley, 1901 census)

Phillis Semen
Baptized Christ Church, Walker, Northumberland, 25 January 1893

Lucy Sex
Born Dorking, Surrey, 1844

William Sexace
Born Brighton, Sussex, c.1825 (South Malling, Sussex, 1851 census)

Mabel Sexey Sexey
Born Stockport, Cheshire, 1893

George Sexy
Born Bakewell, Derbyshire, 1843

Minnie Shafter
Born Hull, Yorkshire, c.1879 (Sculcoates, Yorkshire, 1901 census)

Thirza Shagg
Born Gloucestershire c.1821 (Old Sodbury, Gloucestershire, 1841 census)

Mary A. Shagger
Born Poplar, London, c.1876 (Bromley, London, 1891 census)

Fanny Shaggs
Born Datchworth, Hertfordshire, c.1832 (Hertford, 1851 census)

Titus Shagin
Born Russia c.1875 (Shoreditch, London, 1901 census)

Dick Shagshaft
Born Islington, London, c.1861 (Shoreditch, London, 1881 census)

John Shagshutt
Married Betty Bate, St Peter's Collegiate,
Wolverhampton, Staffordshire, 25 July 1813

Emma Shagwell
Born Brixton Hill, Surrey, c.1828 (Kentish Town, London, 1891 census)

Dick Shaker
Baptized Fenny Compton, Warwickshire, 5 November 1772

Hugh Sin
Married Jane Entwistle, St Laurence, Chorley, Lancashire, 27 February 1738

Enoch Sincock
Buried Breage, Cornwall, 22 November 1818

Ethel S. X. Sinner
Born London c.1876 (St George in the East, London, 1891 census)

Anne Slag
Baptized Hope, Derbyshire, 25 October 1693

Salome Slapper
Born Chipping Sodbury, Gloucestershire, 1891

Virtue Slip
Born Bath, Somerset, 1846

Jane Slut
Baptized Roos, Yorkshire, 28 March 1643

Mary Slutty
Born Birmingham, Warwickshire, 1832

Fanny Smut
Baptized Coldwaltham, Sussex, 4 August 1872

Hester Snogs
Baptized West Hanney, Berkshire,
19 February 1797

Dick Sodom
Baptized Coseley in Sedgley,
Staffordshire, 4 July 1836

G. Spot
(Male) Baptized Edinburgh,
Midlothian, 1 July 1621

Margaret Spunk
Married William Robertson,
St Cuthbert's, Midlothian,
18 May 1812

Amelia Ann Spurting
Baptized St Paul, Deptford, Kent, 5 March 1845

Elizabeth Squirt
Baptized St Mary Whitechapel, London, 27 December 1615

Semion Staines
(Male) Born Maldon, Essex, c.1863 (Maldon, 1871 census)

Benjamin Stiff Stiff
Born Samford, Suffolk, 1893

Enoch Porn Stoner
Born np c.1851 (Bilston, Staffordshire, 1851 census)

Willie Stretch
Born Winsford, Cheshire, c.1894 (Chadderton, Lancashire, 1901 census)

Fanny Stretcher
Born Gloucester 1877

Constable J. Stripper
Born Burnley, Lancashire, c.1872
(Habergham Eaves, Lancashire, 1881 census)

Jane Strips
Born Portsea Island, Hampshire, 1845

Amorous Swain
Died Halifax, Yorkshire, 1843

Fanny Sweetlove
Born Eastry, Kent, 1837

Angelina Swinger
Born Downham, Norfolk, 1879

Hannah Swive
Born Stockport, Cheshire, 1843
*'Swiving' is an Old English term for sexual intercourse. Germaine
Greer once attempted to resurrect its use as a gender-neutral
expression, in the sense that it was a mutual act – people swive
together, rather than a man doing something to a woman –
but it failed to catch on.*

Jane Tarty
Born Biggleswade, Bedfordshire, c.1861 (St George, London, 1881 census)

Wanton Thurston
Married Poplar, London, 1867

Fanny Tickler
Born Withern, Lincolnshire, c.1859 (Grimsby, 1881 census)

Fanny Trollope Tilley
Died Kensington, London, 1851

Kinky Tily
Born Cupar, Fifeshire, Scotland c.1815 (Dundee, Angus, 1851 census)

Melony Tramp
Married Nicholas Williams, Honiton, Devon, 19 April 1742

Fanny Trembling
Born Calne, Wiltshire, 1893

Silly Trollope
Born Doncaster, Yorkshire, c.1894 (Doncaster, 1901 census)

S. Trumpet
(Female) Born Tynemouth, Northumberland, 1862

Semen Tugwell
Born Westonbirt, Gloucestershire c.1794 (Frampton Cotterell, Gloucestershire, 1861 census)

Henry Twiceaday
Married Allice [sic] Crosfield, Aldingham, Lancashire, 17 September 1723

Willie Twitcher
Born Wandsworth, London, 1890

Jane F. Ucker
Born Dunstable, Bedfordshire, c.1801 (Sandy, Bedfordshire, 1871 census)

Jack Ulate
Born Dudley, Worcestershire, c.1835 (Burntwood, Staffordshire, 1861 census)

Alexander Climax Whitehouse
Born Ashton, Warwickshire, 1904

Alice Whore
Married Francis Smyth, Brinklow, Warwickshire, 17 January 1604

Harriot Whore Whore
Born Ross, Herefordshire, 1843

Christiana Whores
Married Johes [sic] Touse, St George, Wilton, Somerset, 25 April 1585

Charles Hardd [sic] Willy
Born Middleton, Yorkshire, c.1880 (Middleton, 1891 census)

Elizabeth Experience Withall
Born Hackney, London, 1856

BRIGHTON GAY, NANCY BOYS AND BIGGERDYKES

George F. Aggot
Born Liverpool, Lancashire, c.1897 (Toxteth, Lancashire, 1901 census)

Bent Beaumont
Born Ashton-under-Lyne, Lancashire, 1845

Barbara Lezza Berrington
Born np 1903; died Windsor, Berkshire, 1984

Liz Bian
Born Hertfordshire c.1786 (Hitchin, Hertfordshire, 1841 census)

Fanny Biggadyke
Baptized Whaplode, Lincolnshire, 24 May 1744

A. Biggerdyke
(Female) Born Moulton, Lincolnshire, c.1809
(Spalding, Lincolnshire, 1861 census)

John T. Bothways
Born Stapleford, Nottinghamshire, c.1856
(Willington, Derbyshire, 1881 census)

Lezzie Box
Born St Luke, Finsbury, London, c.1874 (St Luke, 1891 census)

Nancy Boys
Born Brighton, Sussex, c.1842 (Brighton, 1871 census)

Delita Dyke
Married Matthew Fisher, Alverstoke, Hampshire, 24 November 1844

Emma Dyke Dyke
Born St George Hanover Square, London, 1896

Lesse Dyke
(Male) Born Kemsing, Kent, c.1829 (Kingsdown, Kent, 1851 census)

Thomas Loveless Dyke
Born Poole, Dorset, 1882

Wilfred Titanic Dyke
Born np 1912; died Chorley, Lancashire, 1985

Alfred Want Dykes
Born Hackney, London, 1865

Marmaduke Faggott
Baptized Selby, Yorkshire, 12 November 1797

Lesby Fannawell
Born Shirebrook, Derbyshire (Warsop, Nottinghamshire, 1851 census)

Brighton Gay
Married Helston, Cornwall, 1881

Henry Gay Gay
Born Bedwelty, Monmouthshire, 1884

Sarah Gaybeard
Married Robert Briggs, Westbury on Trym, Gloucestershire, 9 July 1807

Thomas Gaycock
Baptized St Bride's Fleet Street, London, 29 March 1723

Oscar Gaylard
Born Plymouth, Devon, 1884

Mary Anne Gaylove
Baptized Sandy, Bedfordshire, 21 May 1820

Emma G. Gay Guy
Born Lichfield, Staffordshire, c.1831
(Lichfield, 1851 census)

Camp Henry
Born Islington, London, c.1840
(Islington, 1901 census)

Queer Selina Victoria Hert
Born Hamworthy, Dorset, c.1879
(Branksome, Dorset, 1901 census)

Adam Homo
Married Christian Somerval,
Dalziel, Lanarkshire, 27 January 1705

Homo Jones
Born Cardigan 1877

Fanny Sappho Pogson
Born Christchurch, Hampshire, 1886

Roger Poof
Married Elizabeth Brown, Salisbury,
Wiltshire, 4 October 1604

Henry Queer
Born Kirkintilloch, Dunbarton, 7 May 1809

Gayman Rackstraw
Married Wandsworth, London, 1899

Lezza Scragg
Born Burslem, Staffordshire, c.1860 (Burslem, 1861 census)

Albert Gay Sexton
Born Thurning, Norfolk, c.1866 (Thurning, 1871 census)

William Shirtlift
Born Rotherham, Yorkshire, 1859

Joseph Faggot Tempest
Born Houghton-le-Spring, Durham, 1888

M. Vaseline
(Male) Born Le Havre, France, c.1864 (Southampton, Hampshire, 1881 census)

Lesbiana Wharton
Born Ross, Herefordshire, c.1803 (Chelsea, London, 1881 census)

ONE OF THE BUCKINGHAM FUCKINGHAMS?*

Since 'fuck' has been permitted in print only since the Lady Chatterley *trial of 1960, and remains taboo, it is surprising to discover its long-standing use as a personal name.*

Samuel Fucker Chivers
Born Bath, Somerset, c.1809 (Bath, 1861 census)

Emma Fuck Fisk
Died Stepney, London, 1834

Charlotte Fuck
Born np c.1799; died Kingsclere, Hampshire, 1870

Rob Fuck
Born Isle of Man c.1841 (Isle of Man, 1871 census)

Henry Fuckalls
Born Colchester, Essex, c.1815 (Lambeth, London, 1851 census)
His son was also called Henry Fuckalls.

Violet Fuckard
Born Battersea, London, 1900 (Enfield, Middlesex, 1901 census)

Fanny Fucker
Born Wiltshire c.1825 (Salisbury 1851 census)

Mercy Fucker
Born Kent c.1835 (Mayland, Essex, 1861 census)

Willie Fucker
Born Langtree, Devon, c.1859 (Moretonhampstead, Devon, 1871 census)

Dick Fuckett
Married Marie Dore, Shalfleet, Wellow, Isle of Wight, 17 November 1581

Henry Fuckingham
Born Ab Kettleby, Leicestershire, c.1797 (Matlock, Derbyshire, 1851 census)

Harold P. Fuckly
Born Northamptonshire c.1895 (Kettering, Northamptonshire, 1901 census)

Sarah Fuckman
Born Westbere, Essex, c.1815 (Shoreditch, London, 1851 census)

There are no Buckingham Fuckinghams – made you look, though

Charlotte Fucknote
Born Henfield, Sussex, c.1826 (Henfield, 1891 census)

Crolet N. Fuckott
(Female) Born Paddington, London, c.1898 (Paddington, 1901 census)

Lucy Fucks
Married Thomas Ward, Sileby, Leicestershire, 24 July 1757

Sarah Fuckwell
Born Retford, Nottinghamshire, c.1855 (Sheffield, Yorkshire, 1871 census)

Elizabeth Fuk
Born St Olave, Southwark, London, 1877

Minnie Fukins
Born London c.1847 (Aldington, Kent, 1861 census)

Golde Fuks
Married Mile End, London, 1905

Thomas Fukup
Born Blackburn, Lancashire, c.1874 (Hyde, Cheshire, 1901 census)

Bessie Fux
Married Bristol, Gloucestershire, 1896

Sarah Fuxcock
Born London c.1807 (Edgbaston, Warwickshire, 1861 census)

Jane Fuxlonger
Born London c.1803 (Lambeth, London, 1871 census)

Fuck Hunt
(Male) Born np c.1834 (St Mary Newington, Surrey, 1841 census)

Fuk Yu Lee
Born np 1940; died Leeds, Yorkshire, 1991

Andrew Le Fuckinjon de Cadet
Married Elizabeth Blackmore, Chapel of the Holy Trinity,
Middlesex, 12 June 1678

Yau Fuk Man
Born np 1953; died Banbury, Oxfordshire, 1992

Fuckley John Wilkinson
(Female) Born Ferrybridge, Yorkshire, c.1801 (Selby, Yorkshire, 1871 census)

SO LONG, SUCKERS: AN ORAL SURVEY

◆

Dick Blower
Baptized Roxwell, Essex, 19 September 1559

Fanny Blows
Baptized Bassingbourn, Cambridge, 5 August 1860

Vincent Suck Chamberlain
Born Forehoe, Norfolk, 1845

Isuck Chandler
Born Surrey c.1840 (Carshalton, Surrey, 1841 census)

Emily Etta Cock
Born Sleaford, Lincolnshire, 1884

Nora Cock
Born Greenwich, London, 1900

Munch Cox
(Female) Born Devon c.1791 (Ottery St Mary, Devon, 1841 census)

Henrietta Dick
Born Birkenhead, Cheshire, 1900

Fanny Diver
Born Blything, Suffolk, 1838

Rosetta Donger
Baptized St John the Evangelist, Bury St Edmunds,
Suffolk, 5 October 1873

Dick Eater
Born Ruislip, Middlesex, c.1829 (Ruislip, 1851 census)

Fanny Eater
Born np c.1816 (Hampstead, London, 1841 census)

Henrietta Fanny
Born Cheshire c.1860 (St Martin, Cheshire, 1871 census)

Nora Fanny
Born Grantham, Lincolnshire, c.1873 (Leyton, Essex, 1901 census)

Margaret Fellather
Born Acton Dene, Northumberland, c.1875 (Ingleton, Durham, 1891 census)

Fanny Gobble
Born Romford, Essex, 1858

Henry Gobbler
Baptized St Martin, Birmingham,
Warwickshire, 31 May 1787

Dick Gobling
Born Croydon, Surrey, c.1810
(Lewisham, London, 1881 census)

Sarah Godown
Baptized St Dunstan, Stepney,
London, 1 April 1710

Fanny Goodhead
Born Burton upon Trent,
Staffordshire, 1848

Samuel Sucking Gordon
Born Romford, Essex, 1881

Fanny Greathead
Born Birmingham, Warwickshire, 1873

Ellen Good Head
Married Stoke-on-Trent, Staffordshire, 1862

Fanny Lapper
Born Shoreditch, London, 1841

Harriot Orala Laywell
Born Stepney, London, 1840

Fanny Lick
Born Hastings, Sussex, c.1869 (Hastings, 1891 census)

William Lickass
Baptized Chatteris, Cambridge, 13 May 1694

Dick Licker
Born Oldham, Lancashire, c.1845 (Oldham, 1861 census)

Messy Licker
(Female) Born Chorley, Lancashire, c.1803 (Manchester, 1861 census)

Connie Linger
Born Wolverhampton, Staffordshire, c.1889
(Birmingham, Warwickshire, 1891 census)

Dick Muncher
Born Welshampton, Shropshire, c.1838
(Horseman's Green, Flintshire, 1891 Wales census)

Sally Orally
Born Ireland c.1831 (Wolverhampton, Staffordshire, 1861 census)

Rosetta Peniss
Born Kensington, London, 1867

Henrietta Prick
Born Liverpool, Lancashire, c.1845 (St Luke, London, 1871 census)

Suca Prick
Born Reed, Suffolk, c.1753

Roger Rimmer
Baptized St Botolph, Aldgate, London 30 May 1658

Jean Slurper
Born Banffshire c.1821 (Gamrie, Banffshire, 1841 census)

Hyman Suck
Born Leeds, Yorkshire, 1899

Deborah Suckall
Born Leeds, Yorkshire, 1879

Matilda Suckcock
Born Warwickshire c.1840 (Aston, Warwickshire, 1841 census)

Dick Sucker
Baptized Weobley, Herefordshire, 21 January 1719

Ann Suckerman
Married Thomas Cocksedge, Ingham, Suffolk, 16 October 1740

Willie Sucking
Born Elham, Kent, 1882

Rebecca Suckit
Married William Webbe, Burmarsh, Kent, 24 November 1614

Charles William Suckoff
Married Elizabeth Stevens, St Dunstan, Stepney, London,
14 September 1856

Sarah Swallows
Married John Wass, Fishlake, Yorkshire, 1733

Fellat Tidser
Born Essex, c.1835 (Chelsea, 1851 census)

Fanny Tongue
Born West Bromwich, Staffordshire, 31 July 1881

Sucky Trevithick
Born Cornwall c.1903 (St Ives, Cornwall, 1841 census)

Thomas Blows Valentine
Born Aston, Warwickshire, 1861

Eta Willey
Born Upottery, Devon, c.1888 (Upottery, 1891 census)

HOPELESS W. ANKERS

W. Anker
(Male) Baptized Wonersh, Surrey, 28 July 1877

James Masters Bates
Born Daventry, Northamptonshire, 1868

Mastin Bates
(Male) Born London c.1866 (Scredington, Lincolnshire, 1881 census)

Dick Beater
Born Norwich, Norfolk, c.1835 (Wisbech, Norfolk, 1851 census)
*At the time of the census, young Dick Beater was a sixteen-year-old
prisoner in Wisbech jail.*

Willy Beatoff
Born Somerset c.1821 (Yeovil, Somerset, 1841 census)

Dick Handler
Baptized Earls Colne, Essex, 29 December 1585

Wank Hardy
Born Idle, Yorkshire, c.1892 (Idle, 1901 census)

Jack Hoff
Born Thetford, Norfolk, 1910

Grace Tosser Makins
Married Grimsby, Lincolnshire, 1905

Fanny Cock Manuel
Born Feock, Cornwall, c.1828 (Feock, 1861 census)

John Thomas Massage
Married Maria Catharine Bond, Old Church, St Pancras, London, 17 June 1780

Jack Off
Married Sarah Clarke, St Peters, Thetford, Norfolk, 28 December 1773

Jane Panter Onan
Born Potterspury, Northamptonshire, 1890
*Pedants claim that what the Biblical Onan did was not masturbation –
but the* Oxford English Dictionary *defines onanism as 'masturbation'.*

Alfred Henry Pullcock
Born Surrey c.1811 (Brighton, Sussex, 1851 census)

Wanker Sayer
(Female) Born Northallerton, Yorkshire, c.1855 (Northallerton, 1861 census)

Fiddle Sehmens
Born Buckinghamshire c.1821 (Aylesbury, Buckinghamshire, 1841 census)

Willy Stroker
Died Salford, Lancashire, 1872

Dick Tosser
Married Rebaka [*sic*] Tothill, Ideford, Devon, 13 April 1685

Dick Wacker
Born Essex c.1781 (Dagenham, Essex, 1841 census)

Thomas Wank
Born np c.1838; died Chorley, Lancashire, 1886

Willie Harriet Wank
Born Leytonstone, Essex, c.1868 (Wanstead, Essex, 1871 census)
*His surname is bad enough, but he was also given his mother's
first name as his middle name.*

Willy Wanker
Born Angus, Scotland (Dundee, 1841 Scotland census)

Easter Wanking
Baptized Wigmore, Herefordshire, 7 February 1822

Bertram H. Wankwell
Born Bournemouth, Hampshire, c.1900 (Bournemouth, 1901 census)

Chapter Four

PRIVATE

FUNCTIONS

Zacharias Barf
Married Mary Cass, Lythe, Yorkshire, 15 October 1775

Boadicea Belch
Baptized Rickmansworth, Hertfordshire, 2 May 1808

Alfred Ming Belcher
Born Henley-on-Thames, Oxfordshire, 1881

Burp Bendon
Born Somerset c.1771 (Old Cleeve, Somerset, 1841 census)

Selina Bidet
Born Clerkenwell, London, 1839

Evan Toilitt Brown
Born Kensington, London, 1886

Urina Buckett
Born Isle of Wight 1867

Ricard Burpy
Baptized Wesleyan Methodist, Frome,
Somerset, 26 October 1817

Shat Butler
(Male) Born Worcestershire c.1834
(Oswaldslow, Worcestershire, 1841 census)

Farting Clack
Born London c.1863 (Walthamstow, Essex, 1871 census)

Turd Collar
Born Ireland c.1821 (St George Hanover Square, London, 1841 census)

Cornelius Crap
Baptized Pelynt, Cornwall, 28 April 1773

Iron Crapp
Born Idle, Yorkshire, c.1886 (Eccleshill, Yorkshire, 1901 census)

Arthur Brown Crapper
Born Sheffield, Yorkshire, 1867

Shitty Dikins
Born Buckinghamshire c.1828 (Swanborne, Buckinghamshire, 1841 census)

Emete Douche
Married John Mantle, Crewkerne, Somerset, 11 January 1601

Fanny Dribble
Born Mile End, London, c.1836 (Bethnal Green, London, 1901 census)

Latrine Dubois
Born Lewisham, London, c.1890 (Lewisham, 1891 census)

Yelle Minnis Dump
Married Euphan Mitchell, Bo'Ness, West Lothian, 27 December 1660

John T. Dung
Born Coveney, Cambridge, c.1859
(Witcham, Cambridge, 1881 census)

Thomas Fart Everall
Born Atcham, Shropshire, 1842

Dick Fart
Married Susannah Blank, Chivelstone,
Devon, 16 September 1788

Betsey Farting
Born Samford, Suffolk, 1843

Teresa Fartwangler
Born Usk, Monmouthshire, c.1828
(Cardiff, 1871 census)

Mary Ann Fartwell
Born Wellington, Somerset, c.1829
(Thorne St Margaret, Somerset, 1851 census)

Fanny Farty
Born Rock, Worcestershire, c.1842
(Tenbury, Worcestershire, 1861 census)

Manure Ford
Born Rickmansworth, Hertfordshire, c.1831 (Harefield, Middlesex, 1851 census)

P. Freely
(Male) Born Liverpool, Lancashire, 1841

Farty Gladwish
Born Hastings, Sussex, c.1882 (Hastings, 1901 census)

Fanny Gush
Baptized Budleigh Salterton, Devon, 1 November 1871

Toilet Halkyard
(Female) Born Oldham, Lancashire, c.1839 (Northowram, Yorkshire, 1871 census)

PRIVATE FUNCTIONS

Fartina Henwood
(Male) Born Rodbaston, Cheshire, c.1796
(Cheadle, Cheshire, 1851 census)

S. Hit
(Female) Born London c.1862 (Kensington, London, 1871 census)

Emily Spew Hole
Born Barton Regis, Gloucestershire, 1885

Ellen Shitehead Holmes
Born Sheffield, Yorkshire, 1862

Urinal James
(Female) Born Llanllwni, Carmarthenshire, c.1889 (Llanllwni, 1891 census)

Hannah Tinkle Jeffrey
Died Sunderland, Durham, 1838

Pissy Jordon
Born Manchester, Lancashire, c.1894 (Manchester, 1901 census)

Hew Lav
Baptized Wemyss, Fife, 30 October 1687

Willy Leak
Married Marjorie Homer, Rowley Regis, Staffordshire, 1 December 1576

Loo Loo
Born np c.1877; died Greenwich, London, 1904

David Urine Looker
Born Swansea, Glamorgan, 1909

Sarah Pissey Loud
Married Bath, Somerset, 1874

Martha Bog McCall
Born Scotland c.1872 (Hammersmith, London, 1891 census)

William Widdle Moseley
Died Derby 1854

Patience Muck
Baptized St Kew, Cornwall, 1 January 1779

Nathanael [sic] Odour
Married Sophia Chinick, St John the Evangelist, Whitwell-on-the-Hill,
Yorkshire, 18 October 1818

Poo Out
Died Stepney, London, 1888

Gleaner Grace Outhouse
Born Mutford, Suffolk, 1884

Lou Paper
(Female) Born Watford, Hertfordshire, c.1858
(Lambeth, London, 1891 census)

Piss Fisher Parkinson
Born Ireland c.1781 (Holborn, London, 1841 census)

Caroline Eliza Passwater
Born Greenwich, Kent, 1861

Shit Paul
Born np c.1811 (St Marylebone, London, 1841 census)

William Shit Payne
Born St Clement Danes, London, c.1799 (Shoreditch, London, 1861 census)
*'Shit' appears to have been added to the census return as an
afterthought – perhaps he did something to upset the enumerator.*

Ada Pee
Born Hereford 1866

Florence May Pee
Born Aston, Warwickshire, 1895

Thomas Peeless
Married Holborn, London, 1893

Bridget Phlegm
Married Dudley, Staffordshire, 1851

Adeliza Piddle
Baptized Holy Trinity, Gosport, Hampshire, 12 November 1803

Peter Piddle
Baptized Fowey, Cornwall, 2 April 1649

Elizabeth Piss
Married Robert Colt, Aldenham, Hertfordshire, c.1530

Dick Pissing
Baptized St Paul, Canterbury, Kent, 26 May 1705

Penticost Pooe
Baptized Quethiock, Cornwall, 10 June 1576

Sarah Jane Soft Pooer
Born Byers Green, Durham, c.1893 (Byers Green, 1901 census)

Apostle Poop
Died Manchester, Lancashire, 1871

Florence Poopy
Born Yarmouth, Norfolk, c.1875 (Kingston upon Hull, Yorkshire, 1901 census)

William Crapper Potts
Born High Peak, Derbyshire, 1837

Betty Potty
Died Clitheroe, Lancashire, 1870

Frank Privy
Born Devon c.1854 (Horfield, Gloucestershire, 1881 census)

Percilla Puke
Married John Stawslee, Crediton, Devon, 2 February 1673

C. Rap
(Female) Born Bethnal Green, London, c.1831
(Bethnal Green, 1881 census)

Jimmy Riddle
Born Melrose, Midlothian, 19 March 1648

Lou Roll
Born Uxbridge, Middlesex, 1902

Enoch Shite
Born Pelsall, Staffordshire, c.1885
(Pelsall, 1901 census)

Thomas Shitt
Married Anne Eaton, Wellington,
Shropshire, 16 October 1725

Cardilia Shitter
(Female) Born np c.1833
(Fawley, Hampshire, 1841 census)

Gertrude Shitty
Born 'foreign parts' c.1829 (Somers Town, London, 1841 census)

Sarah Sick
Baptized Saxby, Leicestershire, 26 May 1811

Bogs Simons
Died Maidstone, Kent, 1853

Susan Slime
Born Dublin, Ireland, c.1820 (Islington, London, 1881 census)

Atty Sneeze
(Female) Born Ireland c.1838 (Oldham, Lancashire, 1861 census)

Ann Sniff
Baptized St Nicholas, Liverpool, Lancashire, 4 March 1807

Betty Snot
Born Worcestershire c.1796 (Worcester, 1841 census)

Rice Spew
Married Katherine Loughes, St Martin, Worcester, Staffordshire, 1 May 1706

Crink Spittle
(Female) Born Stourbridge, Worcestershire, 1874

Richard Goodluck Spittle
Born Kingston, Surrey, 1903

Brown Spray
Born Thorne, Yorkshire, 1874

Ida E. Sprinkle
Born Slaley, Northumberland, 29 January 1886

Sarah Squit
Married Thomas Wright, St Anne, Soho, London, 8 May 1717

Joshua Stink
Married Mary Bondock, St James, Duke's Place, London, 2 September 1686

Charles Stinker
Died Portsea Island, Hampshire, 1875

Shitty Strange
Born Haselbury, Dorset, c.1844 (Haselbury, 1851 census)

Betty Sweat
Married James Thompson, St Mary, Lancaster, Lancashire, 15 January 1776

Mary Sweaty
Baptized St Mary's, Aylesbury, Buckinghamshire, 27 April 1623

Susan Jane Puke Syms
Born Totnes, Devon, 1844

Mary Tampon
Baptized Somersham, Suffolk, 16 March 1701

Ulalia Tinkle
Married Henry Stephens, Littleham by Bideford, Devon, 29 December 1699

Latrine Topping
Born Warrington, Lancashire, c.1871 (Warrington, 1881 census)

Lancelot Shite B. Tristram
Born St George Hanover Square, London, 1898

Thomas Turd
Baptized St Matthew, Bethnal Green, London, 19 October 1788

Zenobia Urine
Baptized Wendron, Cornwall, 24 May 1799

Sally Vates
Born Billings, Lancashire, 12 August 1764

Thomas Dung Voce
Born Bourne, Lincolnshire, 1842

Sue Wage
Born Wensey, Wiltshire, c.1839 (Lewisham, London, 1891 census)

Ah Wee We
Born np c.1869; died Hartlepool, Durham, 1909

Urinal Welburn
Born Garton, Yorkshire, c.1817 (Great Driffield, Yorkshire, 1881 census)

Fanny Wetter
Born St Austell, Cornwall, 1846

Agnes Widdle
Born Louth, Lincolnshire, 1846

Theophilus Windy
Born Weston, Lincolnshire, c.1830 (Weston, 1891 census)

Maria Wiper
Born Newcastle upon Tyne, Northumberland, 1901

Enema Bottomley Wood
Born np c.1848; died Huddersfield, Yorkshire, 1904

Chapter Five

LOONY LERGY AND LETHAL

CRAZY NAME, CRAZY GUY

———◆———

Elizabeth Barmy
Married William King, Letheringsett, Norfolk, 1702

John Moron Battey
Born Derbyshire c.1879 (Cudworth, Yorkshire, 1901 census)

Lettuce Bedlam
Married James Hill, Nottingham, 10 November 1596

Bernard Daft Butler
Born Prescot, Lancashire, 1907

Daft Coggins
Born Nottingham 1859

Freak E. Cox
(Male) Born Carshalton, Surrey, c.1877 (Carshalton, 1891 census)

Alice Crackers
Born Hull, Yorkshire, c.1871
(St Margaret, Leicestershire, 1891 census)

Ada Crazy
Baptized Thorpe Acre and Dishley, Leicestershire, 4 April 1869

Dick Daft
Baptized St Thomas, Ardwick, Manchester, 2 February 1873

Mary Dope
Baptized Rathkeale, Limerick, Ireland, 17 August 1746

Isaac Dopey
Married Hannah Shaw, Bonsall, Derbyshire, 24 February 1803

Loon Alexander Edgar
Born Eastry, Kent, 1893

Loonie Fattelay
Married Lewisham, London, 1908

Mad Fontheim
Married Hampstead, London, 1903

George Freaky
Baptized Worplesdon, Surrey, 25 December 1814

Nutty Haddock
Died Plomesgate, Suffolk, 1859

Mad Hatter
Born Wigginton, Oxfordshire, c.1879
(Northfield, Worcestershire, 1901 census)
*Coincidentally, Oxfordshire was the location of
Lewis Carroll's* Alice in Wonderland.

Kathleen Psycho Houghton
Born Oxford 1878

Mania Hyman
Born Bethnal Green, London, 1903

John Idiot
Married Hailsham, Sussex, 1848

Maniac Keene
Born Chertsey, Surrey, c.1860 (Chertsey, 1861 census)

Easter Loony
Baptized Maughold, Isle of Man, 11 November 1744

John Loopy
Born Ireland c.1816 (Tadcaster, Yorkshire, 1841 census)

George Mad
Married Jane Cole, Cucklington, Somerset, 1 February 1699

Mary Madcap
Married John Bastard, Wells-next-the-Sea, Norfolk, 9 July 1782

Elijah Madhouse
Born Lye, Worcestershire, c.1816 (Lye, 1881 census)

Temperance Madly
Died Monmouth 1881

Isaac Madman
Married Elizabeth Sewell, St Andrew, Rugby, Warwickshire, 16 November 1811

John Mental
Married Elizabeth Martin, Seaborough, Somerset, 16 January 1609

Lozies Moron
Born Bromsgrove, Worcestershire, 1878

Barm E. Neale
(Male) Born Holloway, London, c.1835 (Hove, Sussex, 1861 census)

Tommy Nuts
Born np c.1833; died Burnley, Lancashire, 1896

Edith Hard Nutter
Died Hackney, London, 1864

Handle Nutter
Born Burnley, Lancashire, 1871

Joyce Moody Nutter
Born np 1925; died Braintree, Essex, 2001

Sugar Nutter
Born Burnley, Lancashire, 1853

Mad Parrott
(Female) Born Piedmont, Italy, c.1821
(St George Hanover Square, London, 1861 census)

Beatrice Retard
Born St Pancras, London, c.1877 (St Pancras, 1881 census)

William Joseph Lunatick Rogers
Married Stepney, London, 1856

Mary Ann Stupid
Born Middlesex c.1821 (St Dunstan in the West, London, 1841 census)

Batty Treasure
(Female) Born Midsomer Norton, Somerset, c.1795
(Midsomer Norton, 1861 census)

MEDICAL MONIKERS

Elizabeth Agony
Married Wrexham, Denbighshire, 1849

Rehab Allwright
(Female) Born Cholsey, Oxfordshire, c.1843 (Cholsey, 1851 census)
Rehab's siblings include Parfet and Quiet.

Margaret Aspirin
Married Noah Wareham, Bowdon, Cheshire, 1 May 1831

Bridget Blackeye
Married Richard Jones, London, 1 May 1617

Jack Acne Blunsden
Born np 1926; died Merton, Surrey, 1988

Clara Spotty Broughton
Born Ongar, Essex, 1843

Charity Clap
Baptized Branscombe, Devon, 11 June 1643

Piles Edycle Cradock
Born Somerset c.1840 (West Derby, Lancashire, 1861 census)

George Typhus Elliott
Married Toxteth Park, Lancashire, 1896

Frances Flu
Married Anne Richardson, Westminster, London, 18 March 1724

Margaret Coma Garland
Born West Bromwich, Staffordshire, 1904

Elizabeth Prettijohn Gleet
Baptized Combe Street Independent, Lyme Regis, Dorset, 24 July 1819
*It is hard to imagine how a word that refers to a discharge associated
with a sexually transmitted disease might also be a surname.*

Hernia Harker
Born Bolton, Lancashire, 1887

Dicky Hart
Born Mile End, London, c.1888 (Bethnal Green, London, 1891 census)

Barbaray [*sic*] Headache
Baptized Wonston, Hampshire, 16 August 1576

Comfort Health
(Male) Born Buckhurst Hill, Essex, c.1828
(Bethnal Green, London, 1871 census)

Henry Hiccups
Born Westbury-on-Severn, Gloucestershire, 1852

Isabella Itch
Married John Heyworth, Newchurch-in-Rossendale, Lancashire, 8 June 1875

Dick Itchcock
Born Huntingdonshire c.1856 (Basford, Nottinghamshire, 1881 census)

Viral Beatice James
Born Wells, Somerset, 1907

James Boil Johns
Born Sherborne, Dorset, 1907

Merrie Leper
Born 'foreign parts' c.1801 (Glasgow Bridegate, 1841 Scotland census)

Martha Lergy
Married Ormskirk, Lancashire, 1865

Syphilla Mears
(Female) Born Exeter, Devon, c.1848 (Exeter, 1881 census)

Samuel Measles
Baptized Welford-on-Avon, Gloucestershire, 8 April 1747

Agony Minchin
Born Bradfield, Berkshire, 1860

Richard Mumps
Born Salford, Lancashire, 1864

John Pox Oliver
Born Yaxley, Huntingdonshire, c.1866 (Yaxley, 1891 census)

Constant Pain
(Female) Born Hackney, London, 1901 (Hackney, 1901 census)

Edward Steady Pain
Born Dover, Kent, 1891

Priscilla Piles
Baptized St Andrew by the Wardrobe, London, 11 February 1736

Mary Pimple
Born Bridport, Dorset, 1852

Emily Frances Plague
Married Stroud, Gloucestershire, 1865

Bessie Pox
Married George Falconer, Gifford, East Lothian, 13 December 1670

Phoebe Puss
Married Joseph Bramble, Boldre by Lymington, Hampshire, 13 January 1786

Cupid Rash
Born Linton, Cambridgeshire, 1852

Dick Rash
Born Chesterton, Cambridgeshire, 1872

Emma Royds
Born Bury, Lancashire, 1854

Levina Sinus
Baptized Holy Trinity-Wesleyan Methodist, Shaftesbury, Dorset,
12 September 1830

R. Sitch
(Female) Born Lambeth, London, 1883

Ann Sneezy
Married Robert Clark Tetford, St Giles without Cripplegate, London,
15 December 1794

Frederick Henry Spasm
Married Prescot, Lancashire, 1894

Mary Ann Squints
Married Shoreditch, London, 1852

Hugh Swelling
Born Ireland c.1811 (Kilbirnie, Ayrshire, 1851 Scotland census)

Hoarse J. Titshall
(Male) Born Letheringham, Suffolk, c.1872 (Dennington, Suffolk, 1881 census)

Prudence Toothaker
Married William Avery, St Olave, Southwark, London, 26 January 1789

Dick Wart
Born Northamptonshire c.1811
(Silverstone, Northamptonshire, 1841 census)

Nerve Wart
(Male) Born Holborn, London, c.1822 (Holborn, 1851 census)

Virus Wheelhouse
(Female) Born Hebden Bridge, Yorkshire, c.1839
(Hebden Bridge, 1901 census)

FROM GRIMWOOD DEATH TO PHIL GRAVES

John Hell Bell
Died West Derby, Lancashire, 1854

Jet Morticia Black
Born np 1961; died Birmingham 1998

John Bury Bury
Born Chorlton, Lancashire, 1846

Mary Carcass
Born Reading, Berkshire, c.1863
('Punch and Judy performer', Horsham, Sussex, 1881 census)

James Cemetery
Died Liverpool, Lancashire, 1844

Samuel Lowery Coffin Coffin
Born Hoo, Kent, 1843

Violet Corpse
Born Whitby, Yorkshire, 1891

Helen A. Deadbody
Born Northamptonshire c.1875 (St John, Cheshire, 1881 census)

Archibald Deadly
Born Paddington, London, c.1875 (St Gregory by Paul's, London, 1891 census)

Grimwood Death
Born np c.1810; died Hartismere, Suffolk, 1884
*Several generations of Grimwood Deaths are recorded, the most
recent (spelling his surname 'De'Ath') dying in 2002.*

Lazarus Death
Born Cambridge 1844

Macro Death
Born Bury St Edmunds, Suffolk, 15 August 1827

Ritzpah Death
(Female) Born London c.1879 (Diss, Norfolk, 1891 census)

Thomas Jolly Death
Died Epsom, Surrey, 1908

Jacob Decay
Married City of London 1861

Daniel Demon
Married Louize Beniel, St James, Duke's Place, London, 10 August 1692

Dominick Doom
Born Somerset, c.1845 (Whitchurch, Herefordshire, 1861 census)

Ann Ghostly
Died Gloucester 1870

Hyatt Ghoul
Born np 1932; died Westminster, London, 2004

Phil Graves
Died Rotherham, Yorkshire, 1879

Fatal Frederick Grucutt
Born Walsall, Staffordshire, 1858

Minnie Hangman
Born Chatham, Kent, c.1882 (Chatham, 1891 census)

Isaac Hearse
Born Axbridge, Somerset, 1852

Christian Killer
Baptized Kinnoul, Perth, 28 September 1784

John Lightning Morgue
Born np c.1809; died St Saviour, Southwark, London, 1884

Mary Murder
Married John Gurrutt, Thurlaston, Leicestershire, 31 December 1881

David Tomb Robb
Born Liverpool, Lancashire, 1845

Sarah Satan
Baptized Layham, Suffolk, 13 September 1778

Stanley Slaughter Slaughter
Born Aylsham, Norfolk, 1893

Lethal Margaret Stothert
Born Castle Ward, Northumberland, 1875

Chapter Six

A GALLIMAUFRY*

OF NAMES

*A dish made by hashing up odds and ends of food; a hodge-podge,
a ragout; a heterogeneous mixture, a confused jumble, a ridiculous medley;
a promiscuous assemblage (of persons)
OXFORD ENGLISH DICTIONARY

Marmalaid [*sic*] Frederick Allen
Born South Shields, Durham, 1885

Ann Apple
Married William Parrott, St Alfege, London Wall, London, 5 May 1792

You say…
Tom Ato
Born Sleaford, Lincolnshire, 1867
I say…
Tom Ayto
Baptized Grantham, Lincolnshire, 28 November 1808

Herodias Pert Bacon
Born Blofield, Norfolk, 1884

Jane Fat Bacon
Born Rippingale, Lincolnshire, c.1811 (Rippingale, 1851 census)

Roy Baguette
Born np 1945; died Cheshire, 2004

Bagel Baker
Born Middlesex c.1816 (Shoreditch, London, 1841 census)

Catherine Banana
Born Barnsley, Yorkshire, 1876

Minnie Bar
Baptized Galston, Ayr, 25 June 1761

Mince Bates
Born Cambridgeshire c.1863 (Bloomsbury, London, 1881 census)

Caroline Isabel Bathbun
Baptized St Mary the Virgin, Reading, Berkshire, 3 May 1846

Rhubarb Bean
Born np 1916; died Bury St Edmunds, Suffolk, 2002

Christopher Strong Beer
Baptized Stoke Damerel, Devon, 17 April 1768

Oliver Beer
Born Salisbury, Wiltshire, 1853

Bertha Bread Binns
Born Wakefield, Yorkshire, 1886

John William Biscuit
Born Oldham, Lancashire, 1870

Jane Bisto
Married Thame, Oxford, 1842
An A. Bisto is also recorded, but not an A.H. Bisto.

Mary Caramel Boot
Born Manchester, Lancashire, 1891

Barbary Booze
Baptized St Mary, Carlisle, Cumberland, 6 June 1686

Maud Stale Bun
Born Sunderland, Durham c.1851 (Sunderland, 1871 census)

Lettuce Burger
Died Bristol, Gloucestershire, 1839

Pleasure Butter
(Female) Born London c.1834 (Holborn, London, 1871)

Christopher Buttermilk
Married Eleanor Walker, Morland, Westmorland, 7 June 1796

Peculiar Buttery
Married Wolverhampton, Staffordshire, 1871

Herbert Cabbage
Born Leyburn, Yorkshire, 1873

Bertha Bacon Cafe
Baptized Stoke-next-Guildford, Surrey, 1 April 1811

Deliverance Smith Cafe
Married Anna Nichols, South Leith, Midlothian, 9 August 1830

Mango Cairns
Died Lambeth, London, 1840

Ambroseus Cake
Baptized Belstone, Devon, 17 October 1613

Harry Eiffel Cakebread
Born St Pancras, London, 1889

Mary Louisa Canape
Born Holborn, London, 1841

Almodad Cheese
Baptized Rochford, Worcestershire, 25 October 1741

Princess May Cheese
Born West Bromwich, Staffordshire, 1896

Charles Chips
Baptized St Dunstan, Stepney, London, 9 October 1808

Sarah Chocolate
Baptized Cranley, Surrey, 14 October 1693,

Agnes Chutney
Born Angus c.1827 (Dundee, Angus, 1841 Scotland census)

Mary Suet Cobley
Born Hastings, Sussex, c.1850 (Hastings, 1851 census)

Cornelius Coffee
Baptized Phillack, Cornwall, 16 November 1868

Pestrop Cola
(Male) Born Barton-upon-Irwell, Lancashire, c.1831
(Barton-upon-Irwell, 1881 census)

Prune Cossey
(Male) Born Mile End, London, c.1874 (West Ham, Essex, 1881 census)

Faithful Christian Cream
Born Chesterton, Cambridgeshire, 1851

Susannah Butter Crease
Born Taunton, Somerset, 1849

Ernest Milk Cremer
Born Norwich, Norfolk, 1876

Walter Cress
Born Cricklade, Wiltshire, c.1858 (Cricklade, 1871 census)

Pleasance Crisp
Baptized Clenchwarton, Norfolk, 22 March 1814

Please Crisp
(Male) Born Suffolk c.1816 (Southwold, Suffolk, 1841 census)

Frances Crumpet
Married Thomas Walters, Tipton, Staffordshire, 5 February 1804

Millie Cucumber
Born Whitechapel, London, 1885

Jam Curry
Married Tiverton, Devon, 1854

Virtue Bible Curry
Born np c.1790; died Thanet, Kent, 1875

Alexander Custard
Baptized Plympton St Mary, Devon, 6 December 1621

William Spam Dadd
Born Skelton, Yorkshire, c.1881 (Skelton, 1901 census)

Happy Wine Dainty
(Female) Born Rugby, Staffordshire, c.1821
(Willenhall, Staffordshire, 1861 census)

Theophilis Tripe Damphey
Born Chard, Somerset, 1862

Louisa F. De la Sausage
Born Kentish Town, London, c.1844 (Enfield, Middlesex, 1871 census)

Al Dente
Born Whitechapel, London, c.1900
(St Botolph, Aldersgate, London, 1901 census)

Lilly Diet
Born Kilwinning, Ayrshire, 2 September 1772

Emily Dinner D. Dinner
Born Launceston, Cornwall, 1906

Ann Drybread
Married Thomas Harberd, St Simon and St Jude,
Norwich, Norfolk, 15 July 1615

Emma Jenefer [*sic*] Egg Egg
Born East Stonehouse, Devon, 1849

Fred Egg
Born Lymington, Hampshire, 1858

Richard Bacon Eggar
Born Alton, Hampshire, 1861

Low Fat
Married Cardiff, Glamorgan, 1905

Philetus Fish
(Male) Born Uxbridge, Middlesex, 1844

Sue Flay
Born Wellington, Somerset, 1871

Colly Flower
Father of Rebecca Flower, born St Anne, Soho, London, 1797

Molasses Frill
Born Londonderry, Ireland, c.1811 (Liverpool, Lancashire, 1861 census)

Melchisedeck Fritter
Married Jone [*sic*] Deane, St James, Clerkenwell Green, London,
26 December 1630

Margarine Fryer
(Female) Born Durham c.1831 (Darlington, Durham, 1841 census)

Gentle Fudge
Stoke Climsland, Cornwall, will, 1662

Normal [*sic*] Cecil Fudge
Born Gloucester 1891

Spencer Puff Gammon
Born Uckfield, Sussex, 1848

Bernard Haggis
Born Barnet, Hertfordshire, 1894

Henry Stunner Ham
Born St Thomas, Devon, 1860

Petronella Hamburger
Born Islington, London, 1876

Spearmint Hardy
Born Blandford, Dorset, 1906

Joseph Aero Hart
Born Rochford, Essex, 1907

George Luncheon Hewitt
Born Greenwich, Kent, 1846

George Raspberry Hogarth
Born Tynemouth, Northumberland, 1898

Lawrence Mash Instance
Born Tendring, Essex, 1871

James Jam
Buried Camborne, Cornwall, 9 August 1772

Eliza Fruit Jarritt
Born Kensington, London, 1868

Kind Jelly
Married Sarah Philips, St Mary, Alverstoke, Hampshire, 17 September 1754

Watercress Joe
(Male) Born np c.1829 (Burslem, Staffordshire, 1881 census)

Apple Jordan
Born Milton, Kent, 1853

Jane Juice
Married Samuel Dawson, Faversham, Kent, 25 February 1676

George Ketchup
Baptized All Saints, Sudbury, Suffolk, 24 January 1803

Edith Mary Hudson Whis Key
Born Lofthouse, Yorkshire, c.1877 (Lofthouse, 1891 census)

Raspberry King
Born Freebridge Lynn, Norfolk, 1853

Cecil De Winton Kitcat
Born Portsea, Hampshire, 1900

Moses Lard
Born Preston, Lancashire, c.1837 (Preston, 1851 census)

Daisy Lasagna
Born np 1907; died Wandsworth, London, 1988

Basil Leaf
Born York 1895

Emmeline Hole Lemon
Born Barnstaple, Devon, 1889

Lemon Lemon
Married City of London 1885

Orange Lemon
Born Kingston, Surrey, 1871

Piggy Liver
Born Lancashire c.1827 (Radcliffe, Lancashire, 1841 census)

Louisa Loaf
Born Middlesbrough, Yorkshire, 1897

Elizabeth Macaroni
Born London c.1810 (Weybridge, Surrey, 1881 census)

Sarah Jane Pant Marrows
Born Caistor, Lincolnshire, 1865

Pretty Mash
(Female) Born Lancashire c.1826 (Preston, Lancashire, 1841 census)

Margaret Coffee Maxwell
Born West Derby, Lancashire, 1893

Tomato May
Born Lambeth, London, 1889 (Lambeth, 1891 census)

Mary Magdalene Milk
Married William Hopkins, St John, Hackney, London, 27 April 1751

Posthumous Mince
Died Greenwich, Kent, 1839

Andrew Cheesy Molt
Born St Albans, Hertfordshire, 1871

Trifle Muddock
Married Hartismere, Suffolk, 1853

Sop Muffin
Born Bedford 1846

Joseph Twaddle Mustard
Born Tynemouth, Northumberland, 1897

Alfred Kipper Negus
Born Redruth, Cornwall, 1887

Carry Apricot Nicholls
Born Kingsbridge, Devon, 1885

Hasshold Nut
Born Leicester 4 February 1731

Hazel Nutt
Born Holborn, London, 1894

Flossie Gross Oats
Born Penzance, Cornwall, 1890

Comfort Offal
(Female) Baptized Welland, Worcestershire, 8 April 1756

Mary Potage Oliver
Born Laceby, Lincolnshire, c.1849 (St James, Lincoln, 1871 census)

Edward Singular Onion
Born Shepton Mallet, Somerset, 1871

George Onion Onions
Born Aberystwyth, Cardiganshire, Wales 1879

Ann Orange
Married William Royston, St Dunstan,
Stepney, London, 30 June 1755

Cinderella Orange
Born Wakefield, Yorkshire, 1843

Lemon Orange
Baptized Newcastle-under-Lyme, Staffordshire, 28 July 1723

P. Orridge
(Female) Born Chesterfield, Derbyshire, 1894

Mary Spangle Osborn
Born Eastbourne, Sussex, c.1886 (Eastbourne, 1891 census)

Frederick Cheese Painter
Born Lambeth, London, 1859

Lucy Pancake
Married Thomas Drew, Deene, Northamptonshire, 30 December 1733

Asher Pasta
Born Twickenham, Middlesex, c.1724

Matilda Peach Peach
Born Yeovil, Somerset, 1882

Agnes Etta Pepper
Born Ipswich, Suffolk, 1881

Gordon Salter Pepper
Born Blything, Suffolk, 1876

Truth Peppercorn
Born Edmonton, Middlesex, 1860

Your Pickles
(Male) Born Todmorden, Lancashire, c.1846 (Todmorden, 1871 census)

Agneta Pie
Baptized Belton, near Epworth, Lincolnshire, 4 July 1562

Raisin Plumb
(Male) Born Cambridgeshire c.1839
(West Wratting, Cambridgeshire, 1841 census)

Cashew Poole
Born Birmingham, Warwickshire, 1877

George Pork
Married Jane Wetlock, Cathedral Church of St Thomas of Canterbury,
Portsmouth, Hampshire, 30 July 1827

Theophilus Porridge
Baptized Gravesend, Kent, 22 September 1752

Florence Gooseberry Pratt
Born Whitechapel, London, 1868

Strawberry E. Presnell
Married St Olave, Southwark, London, 1888

Hephzibah Pudding
Married Newington, London, 1845

Butter Reynolds
Married Mile End, London, 1876

Joseph Rhubarb
Married Elisabeth Steward, St Mary in the Marsh,
Norwich, Norfolk, 10 January 1736

Mary Sandwich Rice
Born Cockermouth, Cumberland, 1874

Hans Sandwich
Born Germany c.1858 (Birkenhead, Cheshire, 1881 census)

Annie Seed
Baptized St John Preston, Lancashire, 17 August 1862

Patti Serrie
(Male) Born Ireland c.1816 (Cadder, Lanarkshire, 1841 Scotland census)

Banana Bill Shaw
Born np 1919; died Lincolnshire 2003

Bovril Simpson
Married West Ham, Essex, 1911

William Souffle
Died Newcastle upon Tyne, Northumberland, 1871

Abraham Soup
Married Agnesse Messenger, Burbage, Leicestershire, 23 January 1606

William Radish Southgate
Born Fincham, Norfolk, c.1833 (Bethnal Green, London, 1861 census)

Sarah Spam
Born Durham c.1760 (Bishop Wearmouth, 1841 census)

Min Spiess
Born Laverton, Gloucestershire, c.1876
(Snowshill, Gloucestershire, 1891 census)

Abraham Spinach
Born Bethnal Green, London, 1889

Martha Stew
Baptized Nantwich, Cheshire, 22 April 1827

Getta Supper
Born St Giles, London, 1905

Jam [*sic*] Organ Sweet
Born Gravesend, Kent, 1892

Eunice Tart
Baptized Brierley Hill, Staffordshire, 6 August 1820

Ambrose Tea
Baptized St Botolph, Aldersgate, London, 16 August 1727

Agnes Semolina Thrower
Born Newcastle upon Tyne, Northumberland, 1889

Len Tills
Born Stockton-on-Tees, Durham, 1905

T. Time
(Male) Baptized Crowle, Lincolnshire, 4 August 1855

Sarah Toffee
Born Gravesend, Kent, c.1862 (Clerkenwell, London, 1881 census)

Thomas Treacle
Born Abergavenny, Wales, c.1874 (Abergavenny, 1881 Wales census)

John Gustavus Trifle
Married St George in the East, London, 1858

Jane Loosemore Tripe
Married City of London 1884

B. Troot
(Male) Born Germany c.1841 (Whitechapel, London, 1871 census)

Whitehead Turnip
Baptized Bolsover, Derbyshire, 31 December 1825

James Coke Twist
Born Prescot, Lancashire, 1852

Delicia Veal
Born Bideford, Devon, 1839

Valkyrien Odour Veal
(Male) Born South Stoneham, Hampshire, 1871

Alborac Vinegar
(Male) Born Wiltshire (Downton, Wiltshire, 1841 census)

Mary Vodka
Baptized St Saviour, York, 21 March 1639

Joseph Waffle
Born Withingham, Lancashire, c.1784
(Walton-le-Dale, Lancashire, 1851 census)

Mineral Waters
Born Shoeburyness, Essex, c.1893 (Shoeburyness, 1901 census)

Charles Cranberry Winfield
Married Gloucester 1850

Salami Wingate
(Female) Born Alford, Lincolnshire, c.1842 (Alford, 1851 census)

Chapter Seven

NATURE OR

TORTURE

BEASTLY NAMES

———◆———

Lewis Lobster Abbs
Born Erpingham, Norfolk, 1884

William Rat Adah
Born Liverpool, Lancashire, 1862

Baboon Dalbert Anson
(Female) Born Scotland c.1844 (Clewer, Berkshire, 1871 census)

Annie Ant
Born Whitechapel, London, 1879

Hercules Anthill
Baptized St Peter Southgate, Norwich, Norfolk, 7 June 1711

Abraham Ape
Baptized Staindrop, Durham, 4 January 1669

Liz Ard
Born Ireland c.1824 (Waltham Abbey, Essex, 1871 census)

Hamster C. Armatys
(Male) Born Clerkenwell, London, c.1853 (Headingley, Yorkshire, 1901 census)

Anne Asp
Married John Tarling, Epping, Essex, 4 September 1655

Adder Attack
Born Hull, Yorkshire, c.1866 (Sculcoates, Yorkshire, 1881 census)

Cockle Ayton
Born Depwade, Norfolk, 1842

Benjamin Baboon
Married Mile End, London, 1897

Diehappy Badger
(Female) Born West Bromwich, Staffordshire, c.1860
(West Bromwich, 1861 census)

Minty Badger
Married Southam, Warwickshire, 1866

Smiley Badger
(Female) Born Napton, Warwickshire, c. 1888
(Southam, Warwickshire, 1901 census)

Mary Balamb
Born np c.1811 (St Giles-in-the-Fields, London, 1841 census)

Savage Beare
Baptized St John, Portsea, Hampshire, 3 September 1795

Large Bee
(Male) Born Nottinghamshire c.1829 (Nottingham, 1891 census)
His son was also called Large Bee.

Ladybird Bingley
Born Kensington, London, 1871

Baby Bird
(Male) Born Shotlow, Norfolk, c.1829 (St Marylebone, London, 1871 census)
An unusual name for a 42-year-old farrier and father of eight children.

Charles Game Bird
Born Holborn, London, 1881

Crapper Bird
Born Bury, Lancashire, 1870

Dicky Bird
Born Edmonton, Middlesex, 1894

Earle Bird
Born Wandsworth, London, 1894

Moggy Birdwistle
Born Middlesex c.1832 (Finsbury, London, 1841 census)

Otter Bloodworth
Died Peterborough, Northamptonshire, 1842

Cod Bohling
Died Whitechapel, London, 1880

Lizard Booth
Born Sheffield, Yorkshire, 1838

John Snail Borrell
Born Chorlton, Lancashire, 1882

Margerie Budgie
Married William Coles, Solihull, Warwickshire, 9 February 1571

Anger Bull
Buried St Dionis Backchurch, London, 22 December 1680

Bastard Bull
Died Plomesgate, Suffolk, 1839

Thomas Bulldog
Born Yorkshire c.1851 (Priest Hutton, Lancashire, 1901 census)

Clara Bunny Bunny
Born St Marylebone, London, 1850

Easter Bunny
(Female) Born Yorkshire, c.1826 (Bradford, Yorkshire, 1841 census)

William Mole Burrow
Born Wellingborough, Northamptonshire, 1853

Fly Burt
Born Plymouth, Devon, 1897

Isaac Worm Butcher
Born Blything, Suffolk, 1843

Violet Mice Butcher
Born Wandsworth, London, 1908

Betty Butterfly
Born Spursholt, Hampshire, 1751

Sir Anthony Wass Buzzard
Born St George Hanover Square, London, 1902

Harris Vole Candle
Born Jersey, Channel Islands, c.1820
(Westbury on Trym, Gloucestershire, 1871 census)

Tom Cat
Baptized St Michael's, Withyham, Sussex, 16 October 1624

Wolf Bear Chalvony
Born St George in the East, London, 1910

Kerrenhappuch Chick
(Female) Baptized Thornecombe, Dorset, 17 March 1756

Quintus Chicken
Married Eliza Gillon, Colchester, Essex, 1878

Richard Chimp
Married Anne Wells, St Albans Abbey, Hertfordshire, 22 April 1679

Ethel Chinchilla
Born Aston, Warwickshire, 1900 (Aston, 1901 census)

Sloth Cleaver
(Male) Born Dunstable, Bedfordshire, 1861 (Dunstable, 1861 census)

Pubens Cockle
(Male) Born Northampton c.1869 (Northampton, 1891 census)

Anna Conder
Born Mile End, London, c.1794 (West Ham, 1851 census)

Claude Crabb
Born London c.1875 (Stratford, London, 1901 census)

Mungo Creature
Baptized Holm and Paplay, Orkney, 2 April 1769

Jane Crocodile
Born np c.1822 (Blandford, Dorset, 1841 census)

Job Pickering Crow Crow
Born Ecclesfield, Yorkshire, 1840

Nightingale Cuckoo
Died Westminster, London, 1838

Jack Daw
Born Bermondsey, London, c.1872 (Bermondsey, 1901 census)

Shark Dawson
Died Bradford, Yorkshire, 1852

Thomas Fox Decent
Born Dover, Kent, 1837

Dorothy Spider De La H. Maddocks
Born Ross-on-Wye, Herefordshire, 1890

Emily Wevil Dennett
Born Nantwich, Cheshire, 1882

Mammallia Dobson
Born Yeadon, Yorkshire, c.1861 (Yeadon, 1881 census)

Elizabeth Dodo
Baptized Bristol, Gloucestershire, 12 July 1738

Sarah Dog
Born St Ives, Huntingdonshire, 1844

Zephaniah Donkey
Baptized St Peter's, Liverpool, Lancashire, 2 April 1827

Jane Ding Dove
Born np c.1827; died Spalding, Lincolnshire, 1898

Ginsel Dragon
Married James Alexander, Erskine, Renfrewshire, 12 June 1759

Donald Duck
Born Edmonton, Middlesex, 1899
Donald Duck was the brother of Rhoda Duck.

Love A. Duck
Born Helmsley, Yorkshire, 1820

Snowdrop Eagle
Born St Olave, Southwark, London, 1894

Charlotte Earwig
Baptized St Mary, Marylebone Road, London, 29 May 1772

Vermin Eastwood
(Female) Born Burnley, Lancashire, c.1841 (Blackpool, Lancashire, 1861 census)

Mammal Edwards
Died Pontypool, Monmouthshire, 1846

Ann Eel
Baptized Watlington, Oxfordshire, 16 February 1812

Fanny Elephant
Born Liverpool, Lancashire, 1908

Elle Fant
Born Durham, 1861

Vixen Faulkner
(Female) Born Edmonton, Middlesex, 1889

Fanny Ferret
Born Bideford, Devon, 1877

Mary Ann Fieldmouse
Married Wolverhampton, Staffordshire, 1877

Fish Fish
Born Salford, Lancashire, 1840

Happy Fish
Died Wangford, Suffolk, 1837

John Pilot Fish
Born Loddon, Norfolk, 1839

Milliner Flea
Married Samuel Jewell, St Mary Magdalene, Taunton,
Somerset, 5 September 1695

Locust Fosburg
(Female) Born Leatherhead, Surrey, c.1887
(Camberwell, London, 1891 census)

Foxy Fox
(Male) Born np 1947;
died Bangor, Caernarvonshire, 1999

Zany Fox
Born St Pancras, London, 1908

William Frog
Born Holborn, London, 1849

Newt Gawthrop
Married North Bierley, Yorkshire, 1901

Gazelle George
Married Flegg, Norfolk, 1873

Merry Gibbons
Died Stepney, London, 1846

Magpie Ginger
Born np c.1849; died Sedbergh, Yorkshire, 1902

George Gnat
Born Norfolk c.1796 (Castle Acre, Norfolk, 1841 census)

Edward James Goat Goat
Born Norwich, Norfolk, 1843

Gertrude Obedience Goose
Born Yarmouth, Norfolk, 1898

Mary Grasshopper
Baptized St Giles without Cripplegate, London, 7 February 1762

Adolfine Grebe
Born St Marylebone, London, 1888

Edwin Bullock Guzzle
Baptized Blakeney, Gloucestershire, 11 March 1826

Thomas Chicken Hair
Born Tynemouth, Northumberland, 1838

John Hamster
Married Elizabeth Pearson, Sheffield Cathedral,
Sheffield, Yorkshire, 2 February 1784

Piggy Hart
Born Chorley, Lancashire, 1852

Joseph Hedgehog
Baptized Bromyard, Herefordshire, 15 January 1745

Bland Herring
Born Caistor, Lincolnshire, 1851

Cycle Herring
Born Madeley, Shropshire, c.1897 (Shifnal, Shropshire, 1901 census)

Rembrandt Herring
Born Downham Market, Norfolk, c.1841 (Battersea, London, 1881 census)

Priscilla Hippo
Baptized St Matthew, Bethnal Green, London, 13 October 1782

Stormy Petrel Hodgson
Born Stepney, London, 1892

Trout Holdsworth
Born Skipton, Yorkshire, 1885

Ass Holmes
Born Skipton, Yorkshire, 1866

Hornet Hunk
(Female) Born West Cowes, Isle of Wight, c.1812
(Northwood, Hampshire, 1881 census)

Moth Hunt
(Male) Born Middlesex c.1821 (Hillingdon, Middlesex, 1841 census)

John Jaguar
Married Wigan, Lancashire, 1878

Larva Beatrice Jeffries
Born Hereford 1892

Lamprey Karney
Born Eastry, Kent, 1838

Ali Katt
(Female) Born Axminster, Devon, c.1819 (Lyme, Dorset, 1871 census)

Don Key
Born Norwich, Norfolk, 1885

Turtle King
Married Sheffield, Yorkshire, 1887

Albatross Louisa Kingston
Born Cookham, Berkshire, 1891

Benjamin Pig Kirkham
Born Boston, Lincolnshire, c.1860 (Boston, 1881 census)

Cat Kitten
Born Lawhitton, Cornwall, c.1820 (Launceston, Cornwall, 1851 census)

Adder Knaggs
Born Stockton-on-Tees, Durham, 1855

Martian Lamb
Born London c.1860 (Woolverstone, Suffolk, 1861 census)

Dolphin Leach
Died Camberwell, London, 1911

John James Leveret White Leveret
Born Leicester 1860

Kitty Litter
Born Martson, Cheshire, c.1839 (Wincham, Cheshire, 1851 census)

Lucina Lizard
Baptized St Dunstan, Stepney, London, 22 April 1717

Mary Lobster
Born Ilkeston, Derbyshire, c.1817 (Ilkeston, 1881 census)

Mole Lory
Born Chertsey, Surrey, 1882

Grizall Louse
Baptized Loudon, Ayr, 4 February 1781

Emu Luckwill
Born Williton, Somerset, 1864

Creature Lugger
Buried Sheviock, Cornwall, 23 May 1613

Pilchard Macksey
(Male) Born Liverpool, Lancashire, c.1871
(Litherland, Lancashire, 1891 census)

Ginger Magpie
Born np c.1849; died Sedbergh, Yorkshire, 1902

Emma Mammal
Born Eldingdon, Warwickshire, c.1834
(Birmingham, Warwickshire, 1851 census)

Rabbit Martin
(Male) Born Hampshire c.1835 (Otterbourne, Hampshire, 1841 census)

Cat Mews
Born np c.1839; died Hexham, Northumberland, 1911

Ming Mole
Born Buckinghamshire c.1781 (Ashendon, Buckinghamshire, 1841 census)

William Scrambler Moles
Born np c.1885; died Kings Norton, Worcestershire, 1909

Winnie Weasel Mollinson
Born Chelsea, London, 1859

Grace Monkey
Baptized Sithney, Cornwall, 3 March 1839

Kitty Moose
Baptized Stourton, Wiltshire, 17 April 1825

Dotty Moth
(Female) Born Warwickshire, c.1889
(Kenilworth, Warwickshire, 1901 census)

Moth John K. Moth
Born Bagworth, Leicester, 1845

Elk Mutter
Born Pitminster, Somerset, c.1856 (Corfe, Somerset, 1901 census)

Pascow Newt
Baptized St Dominick, Cornwall, 17 May 1619

Chimp Norman
Born np 1909; died Dacorum, Hertfordshire, 1999

Blanche Zoo Nules
Born Great Bentley, Essex, c.1862 (Colchester, Essex, 1871 census)

Joseph Bug Nunn
Born Stow, Suffolk, 1841

D. Og
(Female) Born Whitechapel, London, c.1785
(Whitechapel, 1851 census)

Maudlin Orang
Married Isaac Lepley, St Dunstan, Stepney, London, 28 February 1700

Otter Otters
Died Mile End, London, 1868

Ann Owl
Baptized Wellington, Shropshire, 13 August 1797

Beaver Panter
Died Kettering, Northamptonshire, 1849

Fine Orick Parrot
Born Stanbridge, Bedfordshire, c.1851
(Leighton Buzzard, Bedfordshire, 1871 census)

Polly Parrot
Baptized Luddington, Lincolnshire, 21 June 1778

Philomena Mary Pelican
Born 7 April 1920; died Hounslow, London, 1988

Matilda Pigeon Pigeon
Born St Giles, London, 1874

Reuben Toad Pinkney
Born Whitby, Yorkshire, 1847

Sara Pismire
Married St Cuthbert, Bedford, 10 April 1666
A pismire is another word for the common ant.

Benjamin Squirrel Pitt
Born Stockport, Cheshire, 1892

Ostrich Pockinghorn
Married St Stephens by Saltash, Cornwall, 1792

John Possum
Married Elizabeth Roy, Holy Trinity,
Gosport, Hampshire, 23 May 1717

John Prawn
Baptized Kilspindie, Perth, 13 March 1737

Peacock Prettyman
(Male) Baptized St Botolph, Aldgate, London, 18 August 1727

Mary Python
Married George Sephton, Aughton by Ormskirk, Lancashire,
14 September 1818

Henery [*sic*] Racoon
Born Stanford-le-Hope, Essex, c.1831
(Dagenham, Essex, 1881 census)

Fanny Mary Cuckoo Rawbone
Died Lambeth, London, 1837

Annie Rhino
Married Merthyr Tydfil, Glamorgan, 1881

Charles Pelican Roebeuck
Married East Stonehouse, Devon, 1856

Hairby Rook Rook
Born Spilsby, Lincolnshire, 1843

Chris Sallis
Baptized Littleport, Cambridgeshire, 17 November 1804

Porridge Salmon
Born Brackley, Northamptonshire, 1840

Sofa Salmon
Born Dunmow, Essex, 1859

Dinah Saw
Baptized St Lawrence, Chobham, Surrey, 18 October 1818

Thomas Sheep Shanks
Born np c.1796 (Holy Trinity, Coventry, 1841 census)

Charles E. Crunk Shark
Born Scotland c.1874 (Stoke Charity, Hampshire, 1891 census)

Cuckoo Hope Shipperson
Born Barnet, Middlesex, 1891

Sarah Jane Shrew
Baptized St Mark, Dukinfield, Cheshire, 5 December 1847

Isabella Shrimp
Baptized St Stephen Coleman, London, 23 November 1718

Mary Winkle Shufflebotham
Born Macclesfield, Cheshire, 1843

Goat Skippen
Died Wangford, Suffolk, 1858

Jane Skunk
Baptized Ottringham, Yorkshire, 13 August 1570

Sarah Slug
Married Roger Hill, Westbury, Wiltshire, 10 April 1757

Alice Snake
Married Joseph Millard, Thornford, Dorset, 3 June 1621

Jane Perfect Sparrow
Born Mere, Wiltshire, 1859

Mary Spider
Married Mathew Tompson, Grantham, Lincolnshire, 3 July 1732

Joseph Squid
Born St George in the East, London, c.1864
(Bethnal Green, London, 1881 census)

Charity Squirrel
Baptized Swimbridge, Devon, 5 February 1565

Bat Stack
Born Merthyr Tydfil, Glamorgan, 1858

Robert Shuffle Starling
Born Plympton St Mary, Devon, 1845

Sophia Stoat
Born Islington, London, 1879

Symen Swine
Married Katherine Tegue, St Thomas the Apostle,
Exeter, Devon, 2 August 1698

Ann Teater
Born Lamberhurst, Sussex, *c.*1854 (Tonbridge, Kent, 1881 census)

Thomas Tiger
Married Elizabeth Stout, St Mary, Beverley, Yorkshire, 23 December 1694

Jemima Tortoise
Baptized Swafield, Norfolk, 6 April 1794

Horse Browe Trist
Born np *c.*1800; died Godstone, Surrey, 1877

Fanny Pony G. Trubody
Born Bedwelty, Monmouthshire, 1881

Debby Turkey
Married Thomas Jackson, Holy Trinity, Gosport,
Hampshire, 14 October 1805

William Cripes Turtle
Married St Martin-in-the-Fields, London, 1862

Jane Dingo Voisey
Died Pembroke *c.*1806

Darrel Vole
Baptized St Botolph, Colchester, Essex, 6 July 1705

Mary Ann Vulture
Married Caistor, Lincolnshire, 1863

Henry Beast Waddingham
Born Howden, Yorkshire, 1842

Elizabeth Wallaby
Baptized Spennithorne, Yorkshire, 7 March 1780

Noble Wasp
Baptized St Mary at Coslany, Norwich, Norfolk, 27 February 1773

Alice Weasel
Born Poplar, London, 1880

Brightweed Whale
Baptized Lezant, Cornwall, 28 January 1585

Clement Sparrow Wham
Baptized Nardwell, Suffolk, 7 November 1839

Mary Ape Wild
Born Wolverhampton Staffordshire, c.1834 (Wolverhampton, 1871 census)

Wildgoose Wildgoose
(Male) Born Bakewell, Derbyshire, c.1846 (Bakewell, 1851 census)

Eliza Auroch Willet
Born Dulwich, London, c.1829 (Lambeth, London, 1901 census)
*The auroch was a cow-like animal that once roamed
across Europe, but became extinct in 1627.*

Hamlet Winkle
Baptized Burslem, Staffordshire, 1 May 1808

Dodo Woodcock
Married Atcham, Shropshire, 1903

Unity Worm
Married John Speller, Salcombe Regis, Devon, 4 November 1805

Margaret McOstrich Yeoman
Born Camberwell, Surrey, 1886

Alice Zebra
Married Westminster, London, 1864

———◆———

FLORA BRITANNICA

Leafy Babb
Died Bideford, Devon, 1904

Blossom Bassam
Born Maidstone, Kent, 1892

Margarett [*sic*] Beanblossom
Born Finsbury, London, 1826; died 1903

Holly Berry
Born Barnsley, Yorkshire, 1880

Pete Bog
Married Eliza Young, St Pancras, London, 1812

Flowery Bolliski
Died Leeds, Yorkshire, 1875

Olive Branch
Born West Ham, Essex, 1880

Rose Bush
Born Shoreditch, London, 1864

Elegant Verbena Edwards
Born Thetford, Norfolk, 1902

Jeannie Machine Flower
Born Scotland c.1859 (Surbiton, Surrey, 1901 census)

Oleander George Freestone
(Male) Born Cambridgeshire c.1849 (Cambridge, 1861 census)

Field Flowers Goe
Born Coningsby, Lincolnshire, c.1798
(Louth, Lincolnshire, 1861 census)

Sophia Grass Grass
Born Thetford, Norfolk, 1862

Ever Green
Born Lexden, Essex, 1847

Theresa Green
Baptized Motcombe, Dorset, 23 September 1804

Sycamore Hyam
Married City of London 1878

Arminel Lavender
Offerton, Cheshire, will, 1812

Vine Leaf
Born York 1896

Dan D. Lyons
Born Cardiff, Glamorgan, 1891 (Cardiff, 1891 census)

Innocent Mandrake
Married Magdalene Young, St George, Mayfair, London, 17 March 1753

Lavender Marjoram
Born Mitford, Norfolk, 1848

Pete Moss
Baptized Acton by Nantwich, Cheshire, 22 June 1679

Dahlia Zsta [*sic*] Norris
Born West Ham, Essex, 1890

Sunny Orchard
Died Poole, Dorset, 1837

Pansy Daffodil Parcell
Born South Stoneham, Hampshire, 1902

Flora Plant
Born Walsall, Staffordshire, 1870

Lawn Ridding
Born Keighley, Yorkshire, 1880

Seaflower Rolls
Born Cookham, Berkshire, 1875
Seaflower was the sister of Benbow, Bluebell, Daisy, May,
Ocean and Snowdrop Rolls.

Calculus Sage
Born Foleshill, Warwickshire, 1901

Cyril Cactus Scott
Born Lewisham, London, 1909

Mitchell Big Tree
Born Chorlton, Lancashire, 1896

Sarabelle Tulip
Born St Marylebone, London, c.1850 (Rotherhithe, London, 1891 census)

Docitheus Twigg
Born np c.1792; died Aston, Warwickshire, 1874

Chapter Eight

BY ACCIDENT

OR DESIGN

SIGN HERE, PLEASE (IF THERE'S ROOM)

◆

Ded Jarvis Blue Adams Handcock Amesbury
Died Bridgewater, Somerset, 1859

Xenophilus Epaphreditus Baycock Calvert
Died Huddersfield, Yorkshire, 1842

Zaphnathpaaneah Isaiah Obededom Nicodemus Francis Edward Clarke
Baptized Beccles, Suffolk, 14 October 1804

Only Francis Edward would fit in the parish register, so the other names were added as a footnote. In 1877 it was reported that 'Mr Zaphnath-Paaneah Isaiah Obed-Edom Nicodemus Francis Edward Clarke, a bloater merchant at Lowestoft, has been poisoned by taking a lotion in mistake for a draught.'

La Rhennee Le Veghonora Jannette Betsey Restall De Louth
Born Midhurst, Hampshire, 1850

Gilbert Edward George Lariston Elliot-Murray-Kynynmound
6th Earl of Minto, 1928–2005

Alaric Fetherstonhaugh-Frampton
Born Kensington, London, 1900

On its own, Fetherstonhaugh is claimed to be the longest unhyphenated English surname. In 1781 Sir Harry Fetherstonhaugh (1754–1846) had as his mistress Emma Hart, later to achieve fame as Emma Hamilton.

Shadrach Meshach Abednego Daniel Goldsmith
Died Stow, Suffolk, 1849

Albrecht Franz Joseph Carl Friedrich Georg Hubert Maria Hapsburg-Lothingen
Archduke of Austria, Prince of Hungary, married Irene Dora Rudnay, Brighton, East Sussex, 16 August 1930

Amy Elizabeth Ezeerd Copah Cash Macintosh
Born Dover, Kent, c.1891 (Shoeburyness, Essex, 1891 census)

Xenia Marelina Veronique Caroline Sophia Murray Moore
Born Richmond, Surrey, 1888

Thomas Hill Joseph Napoleon Horatio Bonaparte
Swindlehurst Nelson
Born Preston, Lancashire, 1839

Tracy Mariclaire Lisa Tammy Samantha Christine
Alexandra Candy Bonnie Ursula Zoe Nichola
Patricia Lynda Kate Jean Sandra Karren Julie Jane
Elizabeth Felicity Gabriella Jackie Corina Constance
Arabella Clara Honor Geraldine Giona Erika
Fillippa Anabel Elsie Amanda Cheryl Alanna Louise
Angie Beth Crystal Dawn Debbie Eileen Grace
Susan Rebecca Valerie Kay Lena Margaret Anna
Amy Carol Bella Avril Ava Audry Andrea Daphne
Donna Cynthia Cassie Christable Vivien Wendy
Moira Jennifer Abbie Adelaide Carissa Clara Anne
Astrid Barbara Clarissa Catalina Bonny Dee Hazel
Iris Anthea Clarinda Bernadette Cara Alison Carrie
Angela Beryl Caroline Emma Dana Vanessa Zara
Violet Lynn Maggie Pamela Rosemary Ruth
Cathlene Alexandrina Annette Hilary Diana
Angelina Carrinna Victoria Sara Mandy Annabella
Beverley Bridget Cecilia Catherine Brenda Jessica
Isabella Delilah Camila Candice Helen Connie
Charmaine Dorothy Melinda Nancy Marian Vicki
Selina Miriam Norma Pauline Toni Penny Shari Zsa
Zsa Queenie Nelson
Born Chesterfield, Derbyshire, 31 December 1985

Maria de los Dolores Petrona Ramona Juana
Nepomucena Josefa Cayetana Beatriz de la
Santisima Trinidad North
Born np c.1811; died Lambeth, London, 1890

Ann Bertha Cecilia Diana Emily Fanny Gertrude
Hypatia Inez Jane Kate Louisa Maud Nora Ophelia
Quince Rebecca Starkey Teresa Ulysis Venus
Winifred Xenophen Yetty Zeus Pepper
Born in West Derby, Lancashire, 19 December 1882
*She was given a name for each letter of the alphabet, except that of
her surname, in alphabetical order.*

The Honourable Sir Reginald Aylmer Ranfurly Plunkett-Ernle-Erle-Drax

Born London 28 August 1880; died Poole, Dorset, 16 October 1967

Charles Caractacus Ostorius Maximillian Gustavus Adolphus Stone

Baptized Burbage, Wiltshire, 29 April 1781

Mahershalalhashbaz Sturgeon

Born Hessett, Suffolk, c.1857 (Hessett, 1881 census)

Mahershalalhashbaz is the longest personal name in the Bible.

Richard Plantagenet Campbell Temple-Nugent-Brydges-Chandos-Grenville

Born 10 September 1823; died London, 26 March 1882

*The 3rd Duke and 4th Marquis of Buckingham; after him
the title became extinct.*

Tollemache-Tollemache

*The Reverend Ralph William Lyonel Tollemache (1826–1895)
was rector of South Wytham, near Grantham, Lincolnshire.
His first wife was his cousin Caroline Tollemache (1828–1867),
with whom he had five children:*

Lyonel Felix Carteret Eugene Tollemache (1854–1952)

Florence Caroline Artemisia Hume Tollemache (1855–1935)

Evelyne Clementina Wentworth Cornelia Maude Tollemache (1856–1919)

Granville Gray Marchmont Manners Plantagenet Tollemache (1858–1891)

Marchmont Murray Reginald Grasett Stanhope Plantagenet Tollemache (1860–1898)

*Following the death of his first wife, in 1869 he married Dora
Cleopatra Maria Lorenza de Orellana y Revest (c.1847–1929) and
got into his naming stride with their ten children:*

Dora Viola Gertrude Irenez de Orellana Dysart
Plantagenet Tollemache-Tollemache (1869–1874)

Mabel Helmingham Ethel Huntingtower Beatrice
Blazonberrie Evangeline Vise de Lou de Orellana
Plantagenet Saxon Toedmag Tollemache-Tollemache
(1872–1955)

Lyonesse Matilda Dora Ida Agne Ernestine Curson
Paulet Wilbraham Joyce Eugénie Bentley Saxonia
Dysart Plantagenet Tollemache-Tollemache
(1874–1944)

Lyulph Ydwallo Odin Nestor Egbert Lyonel Toedmag
Hugh Erchenwyne Saxon Esa Cromwell Orma
Nevill Dysart Plantagenet Tollemache-Tollemache
(1876–1961)
The initial letters of his first names spell 'Lyonel the Second'.

Lyona Decima Veronica Esyth Undine Cyssa Hylda
Rowena Viola Adela Thyra Ursula Ysabel Blanche
Lelias Dysart Plantagenet Tollemache-Tollemache
(1878–1962)

Leo Quintus Tollemache-Tollemache de Orellana
Plantagenet Tollemache-Tollemache (1879–1914)
*In 1908 he renounced all but the first and last of his
extravagant names by deed poll.*

Lyonella Fredegunda Cuthberga Ethelswytha Ideth
Ysabel Grace Monica de Orellana Plantagenet
Tollemache-Tollemache (1882–1952)

Leone Sextus Denys Oswolf Fraudatifilius
Tollemache-Tollemache de Orellana Plantagenet
Tollemache-Tollemache (1884–1917)

Lyonetta Edith Regina Valentine Myra Polwarth
Avelina Philippa Violantha de Orellana Plantagenet
Tollemache-Tollemache (1887–1951)

Lynonulph Cospatrick Bruce Berkeley Jermyn
Tullibardine Petersham de Orellana Dysart
Plantagenet Tollemache-Tollemache (1892–1966)

Henry Edward Montague Dorington Clotworthy Upton
Born Kensington, London, 1853
On the death of his uncle in 1890, he became Viscount Templeton.

Kiscernotta Corniella Sling Kend Whittaker
Born Netherlands, British subject, c.1864
(Poulton-le-Fylde, Lancashire, 1901 census)

Dancell Dallphebo Marc Antony Dallery Gallery Caesar Williams
Baptized Old Swinford, Worcestershire, 28 January 1676
Son of Dancell Dallphebo Marc Antony Dallery Gallery Caesar Williams.

———◆———

PURITAN NAMES

Even biblical names were not considered sufficiently pure by Puritan extremists, so they gave their children 'virtue' names such as Humiliation and Mercy, or slogans (Fly-fornication, Seek-wisdom, et al). They were especially prevalent in Kent, Sussex and Northamptonshire. Among Sussex Puritans, in the parish of Warbleton, almost half the children baptized between 1570 and 1600 received such names. A few girls' names, including Felicity, Joy and Prudence, have survived in the British name stock, but most have not.

Fly-fornication Andrewes
Baptized Waldron, Sussex, 17 December 1609
'Bastard son of Catren Andrewes.'

Nicholas If-Jesus-Christ-Had-Not-Died-For-Thee-Thou-Hadst-Been-Damned Barebon
Born London c.1640; died Osterley, Middlesex, 1698
Son of Praise-God Barbon (after whom the 'Barebones Parliament' was named) and, following the Great Fire of London in 1666, inventor of fire insurance. He used the name Nicholas Barbon.

Magnify Beard
Baptized Warbleton, Sussex, 17 September 1587

Lament Bible
Married Nicholas Hussher, Ticehurst, Sussex, 9 September 1640

Mercye Bike
Baptized Thornhill by Dewsbury, Yorkshire, 9 February 1651

Fear Brewster
Born Scrooby, Nottinghamshire, c.1586

Fear and her siblings Patience, Love and Wrestling were among the 'Pilgrim Fathers' who emigrated to America in 1620 aboard the Mayflower. *She died in Massachussetts on 12 December 1634. US President Zachary Taylor was a descendant of Fear. The* Little Women *author, Louisa May Alcott, the singer Bing Crosby and the actress Katharine Hepburn were all Brewster descendants.*

Repent Champney
Baptized Warbleton, Sussex, 14 August 1608
'A bastard.'

Clemency Chawncey
Buried St Dionis Backchurch, London, 27 August 1625

Be-Courteous Cole
Born Pevensey, Sussex, 1570

Changed Collins
(Female) Born Brightling, Sussex, 1 January 1598
She was the sister of:

Increased Collins
Born Brightling, Sussex, 30 March 1604

Redeemed Compton
Born Battle, Sussex, 1588

Diligence Constant
Buried St Peter upon Cornhill, London, 1 November 1724

God-help Cooper
Baptized Weybridge, Surrey, 12 June 1628

Sorry-for-sin Coupard
Baptized Warbleton, Sussex, 25 January 1589

Abuse-not Ellis
Baptized Warbleton, Sussex, 17 September 1592

Preserved Emms
(Female) Died St Nicholas, Yarmouth 17 November 1712

More-fruit Fenner
Baptized Cranbrook, Kent, 22 December 1583
*Dudley Fenner (c.1558–1587), preacher of Romford, Essex, was
accused of baptizing children with such names as Joy-again and
From-above, but defended himself by pointing out that he had given
his own daughters the names More-fruit, Faint-not and Dust.*

Replenish French
Baptized Warbleton, Sussex, 13 May 1660

Accepted Frewen
Baptized Northiam, Sussex, 26 May 1588; died 28 March 1664
*Accepted Frewen, brother of Thankfull Frewen (born Northiam,
Sussex, 1591, died 1656), became Archbishop of York.*

Joy-in-sorrow Godman
Married Joseph Baysie, All Saints, Lewes, Sussex, 20 May 1614

Hate-evil Greenhill
Baptized Banbury, Oxfordshire, 15 April 1660

Sin-deny Hely
(Female) Married William Swane, Burwash, Sussex, 4 September 1621

Humiliation Hinde
Married Elizabeth Phillips, St Peter upon Cornhill, London, 24 January 1629

Safe-on-high Hopkinson
Baptized Salehurst, Sussex, 28 February 1591

Job-rakt-out-of-the-asshes [*sic*]
(Foundling) Baptized St Helen, Bishopsgate, London, 1 September 1611

First-borne and Sadness Luffe
(Female twins) Baptized Aylesbury, Buckinghamshire, 2 September 1656

Free-gift and Fear-not Lulham
(Male twins) Baptized Warbleton, Sussex, 12 October 1589

Aydonhigh Mutlow
(Male) Baptized Bosbury, Herefordshire, 22 November 1601
The brother of:

Abstinence Pougher
(Male) Baptized St Nicholas, Leicester, 30 June 1672

More-fruit Stone
(Male) Baptized Alfriston, Sussex, 6 June 1587
The father of:

Zealous Stone
(Male) Baptized Hellingley, Sussex, 8 March 1612

No-merit Vynall
(Female) Baptized Warbleton, Sussex, 28 September 1589

Continent Walker
(Female) Baptized Alfriston, Sussex, 22 December 1594

Discretion Watkinson
Married Elizabeth Wild, South Muskham, Nottinghamshire, 17 November 1659

Restored Weekes
Married Constant Sumar, Chiddingly, Sussex, 27 August 1618

Faint-not Wood
Married William Clarke, Laughton, Sussex, 24 December 1618

Repentance Wrath
(Male) Baptized Elham, Kent, 26 March 1612

Rejoice Wratten
(Female) Baptized Warbleton, Sussex, 18 October 1679

THICKIES, BASTARDS AND BITCHES

◆

Many of the names in this book are bad enough, but imagine having to live with one that is, or sounds as if it might be, pejorative or downright insulting.

Blooming Alexander
Born Plymouth, Devon, c.1816 (Plymouth, 1851 census)

Nosy Allen
Born St Clement, Oxford, c.1883 (St Clement, 1891 census)

B. Astard
(Male) Born Staffordshire c.1826 (West Bromwich, Staffordshire, 1841 census)

Fatty Atkinson
(Male) Born Hull, Yorkshire, c.1868
(Kingston upon Hull, Yorkshire, 1881 census)

Elizabeth Awkward
Married Bury, Lancashire, 1866

Bag Carolin [*sic*] Bagley
Married Southampton, Hampshire, 1861

Hannah Banal
Born np c.1806 (Clifton, Derbyshire, 1851 census)

Ellen Ferran Bastard Bastard
Born Walsingham, Norfolk, 1846

Lucretia Bastard
Born Crowan, Cornwall, 20 June 1700

Friendless Baxter
Born Holbeck, Yorkshire, 1871

Shouvaveva J. Berk
Died Bromley, Kent, 1910

Xpoferus Berk
(Male) Married Aliciam Browne, Gillingham,
Dorset, 18 November 1661

Patrick Bighead
Died Chorlton, Lancashire, 1864

Maryan Bitch
Married Taunton, Somerset, 1840

A. Blob
(Female) Born Yorkshire c.1827 (Snaith, Yorkshire, 1841 census)

Philip Percy Bonehead
Married Bedminster, Somerset, 1895

David Twitty Boocock
Born Adlington, Cheshire, 1855

Mary Boring
Born West Derby, Lancashire, 1857

P. George Hopeless Bradbury
Born Sheffield, Yorkshire, 1874

Dick Brain
Born Stoke-on-Trent, Staffordshire, 1871

Porker Braybrook
Died Sudbury, Suffolk, 1845

James Crummy Brewis
Married Tynemouth, Northumberland, 1842

Frightful Brown
Born np c.1886 (Attercliffe, Yorkshire, 1871 census)

John Dull Brown
Born West Derby, Lancashire, 1888

Hannah Buffoon
Born np c.1793; died Stockton-on-Tees, Durham, 1872

Lousy Butler
Born Bradford, Yorkshire, 1885

Eleanor Misery Charlotte
Born Stepney, London, 1873

Thomas Chav
Married Jane Parkinson, St John's, Preston, Lancashire, 30 January 1867

Charles Daffy Child
Born Dewsbury, Yorkshire, 1899

Louise Emma Clot
Married Westminster, London, 1903

Nasty Clough
(Male) Born Yorkshire c.1786 (Bowdon, Cheshire, 1861 census)

George James Cockhead Cockhead
Born St George in the East, London, 1860

George Cokehead
Married Ware, Hertfordshire, 1839

Thomas Creep Collingwood
Born Islington, London, c.1852 (Kensington, London, 1871 census)

Seedy Mary Cooper
Born Llanelli, Monmouthshire, 1901

Wanton Coward
(Male) Born Warminster, Wiltshire, c.1863 (Warminster, 1871 census)

Cruel John Crane
Born Shropshire c.1885 (Shifnal, Shropshire, 1891 census)

Justa Crook
(Female) Born London c.1855 (Mile End, London, 1901 census)

Fanny Crud
Born St Marylebone, London, c.1855 (Rotherhithe, London, 1881 census)

Evil Dennis
Born Llanelli, Carmarthenshire, 1884

Blanche Despot
Born St Marylebone, London, c.1867 (Willesden, Middlesex, 1901 census)

Mary Dirty
Baptized St Martin-in-the-Fields, London, 8 November 1685

Charles Dismal
Born Greenwich, Kent, 1858

Thomas Dizzy
Married Elizabeth Wright, St Giles, Reading, Berkshire, 19 October 1740
She thus became Lizzie Dizzy.

Lucy Drip
Baptized Shirley, Warwickshire, 10 November 1833

Richard Drivel
Baptized St Botolph, Aldersgate, London, 28 October 1666

Hubert Drunk
Born Chelsea c.1835 (Stretford, Lancashire, 1861 census)

Reginald Daisy Dull
Born St George Hanover Square, London, 1878

Hanora Dummy
Born Cork, Ireland, 13 May 1878

Dora Dunce
Born Chertsey, Surrey, 1877

Goon Eccles
(Male) Born Pimlico, London, c.1841 (Chelsea, 1891 census)

Weakly Ekins
Inquisition of Lunacy, London, 6 July 1697

Hopeless Evans
Born Stoke-on-Trent, Staffordshire, 1880

Will Fail
Baptized Dunblane, Perthshire, 21 March 1708

Martha Fat
Married Richard Chalkwright, Cathedral Church of St Thomas of Canterbury,
Portsmouth, Hampshire, 16 June 1703

George Fatman
Born Broadbottom, Cheshire, c.1893 (Harefield, Middlesex, 1901 census)

Hugh Fatty
Born Flint c.1790 (Leadbrook Major, Flintshire, Wales 1851 census)

Fanny Fecker
Born Suffolk c.1841 (Bardwell, Suffolk, 1841 census)

Harriet Mann Fiend
Baptized St John the Baptist, Shoreditch, London, 24 March 1839

Charles Filth
Baptized Putney, London, 3 August 1737

Thomas Flop
Married Martha Burges, Wells, Somerset, 25 October 1632

Rich Fool
Married Isabella Dicconson,
Chorley, Lancashire, 24 December 1703

Dolt Fretwell
Born Wortley, Yorkshire, 1890

Fanny Fright
Married Faversham, Kent, 1859

Henry Small Fry
Born Bloxworth, Dorset, 1862 (Bloxworth, 1881 census)

George Garbage
Baptized St Thomas, Dudley, Worcestershire, 7 December 1823

William Nicholas Geek
Born Tavistock, Cornwall, 1848

Richard Gibberish
Married Sarah Manninghe, Poling, Sussex, 22 November 1678

George Gimp
Baptized Axminster, Devon, 26 February 1769

Augusta S. Git
Born Finsbury, London, c.1811 (Islington, 1881 census)

Herbert Blasted Grace
Born Romsey, Hampshire, 1879

John Pest Grimshaw
Born Preston, Lancashire, 1885

Hannah Grubby
Married Thomas Lenn, St Mary Magdalene, Lincoln, 20 May 1787

Barbary Hag
(Female) Baptized Haddington, East Lothian, 13 October 1667

Nasty Elizabeth Halsey
Born Berkhamsted, Hertfordshire, 1882

Lazy Harris
Born West Derby, Lancashire, 1903

Dick Head
Born Wandsworth, London, 1890

Odious Heaton
Died Halifax, Yorkshire, 1888

Abraham Mouldy Herman
Born Wallingford, Berkshire, 1864

Bother Hislop
(Female) Born Midlothian, Scotland, c.1806
(Edinburgh, 1841 Scotland census)

Clotworthy Hoare
Born Kent c.1837 (Blackheath, Kent, 1841 census)

Spoilt Eliza Hobbs
Born Huntington 1871

Dork Holmes
Born Huddersfield, Yorkshire, 1905

James Greasy Holmes
Died Hoxne, Suffolk, 1856

Dorothy Horrible
Married Jeremiah Ford, Fleet Prison, London, 20 May 1733

Nelly Horrid
Baptized Fawley, Hampshire, 29 April 1786

Immanuel Horror
Baptized Acklam, Yorkshire, 4 June 1826

Berk Hunt
Born St Pancras, London, c.1898 (St Pancras, 1901 census)

Rock Idle
Born Dewsbury, Yorkshire, 1873

Eliza Inane
Baptized St Margaret's, Leicester, 2 February 1820

George Joyless
Baptized Manchester Cathedral, Manchester, Lancashire, 7 June 1795

Friggin Lawer
Married Freebridge Lynn, Norfolk, 1838

Vanity Lawrence
Born Chipping Sodbury, Gloucestershire, 1845

Grace Less
Married William Gifford, Taunton, Somerset, 8 September 1738

John Liar
Married Kesia Pryer, St Olave, Southwark, London, 18 October 1765

Scary Looker
(Female) Born Warrington, Lancashire, c.1841 (Warrington, 1851 census)

Niphena Loser
Born np c.1816 (Zeal Monachorum, Devon, 1841 census)

Jeremiah Lousy
Born Boherboy, Cork, Ireland, 25 April 1866

Vandal Mason
Born Wirral, Cheshire, 1895

Dim McTavish
Born Argyll c.1849 (Argyll, 1851 Scotland census)

Grace Banshee Merchant
Born Elham, Kent, 1888

Gustavus Berk Middleditch
Born Bury St Edmunds, Suffolk, 1876

Ditsy Millard
(Female) Born Land's End, Cornwall, c.1876
(West Moors, Dorset, 1901 census)

Strange Milliner
(Male) Married Emma Moore, Faversham, Kent, 1859

Fanny Minger
Born Fishersgate, Sussex, c.1881 (Fishersgate, 1891 census)

Marget [*sic*] Morose
Married Thomas Slacke, Belchamp Walter, Essex, 23 September 1610

Gwen Sod Mortimer
Born St Saviour, Southwark, London, 1845

Libertine Moss
Married Ashton-under-Lyne, Lancashire, 1855

Otto Naff
Died Bethnal Green, London, 1910

Charles Henry Nerd
Baptized St Nicholas, Gloucester, 1 May 1831

Betty Nit
Married Robert Hooper, Westbury, Wiltshire, 9 July 1764

Young Nogood
(Female) Born Newbury, Berkshire, c.1838 (St Giles, London, 1861 census]

Rude Nolan
Married Gravesend, Kent, 1857

Lonely Jack Overton
Born Bosmere, Suffolk, 1903

James Royal Payne
Married Braintree, Essex, 1897

Margaret Perve
Born Kelvedon, Colchester, Essex, c.1519

A. Pervert
(Female) Married George Kelway, Yeovil, Somerset, 15 April 1816

Harry Terrible Phillips
Born St Pancras, London, 1899

Fred Pillock
Baptized Eastrington, Yorkshire, 2 February 1862

Philip Plonker
Baptized Shalford, Surrey, 3 June 1632

Pedro Ponce
Baptized Mitford, Northumberland, 22 August 1885

A Bunch of Pratts

Alfred Pratt Pratt
Born Chipping Norton, Oxfordshire, 1908

Arkless Pratt
(Male) Born Haswell, Durham, c.1863 (Haswell, 1881 census)

Emo Pratt
(Female) Born Lamorlaye, Oise, France, c.1869
(Newmarket, Suffolk, 1871 census)

Horace Jealous Pratt
Born Huntingdon 1883

John Gash Pratt
Born Lincoln 1874

Mystery Pratt
Born np c.1856; died Dewsbury, Yorkshire, 1893

Oswald Beagle Pratt
Born Great Yarmouth, Norfolk, 1879

Failure Radley
Born Lambeth, London, 1864

Whalebelly Robert
Born Saham Toney, Norfolk, c.1818 (Saham Toney, 1861 census)

Robert Rubbish
Baptized St Olave, Southwark, Surrey, 23 August 1702

Fanny Scum
Baptized Calstock, Cornwall, 1805

Dorothy Villain Seymour
Born Islington, London, 1903

Harris Shifty
Born Russia c.1875 (Mile End, London, 1901 census)

Elizabeth Bastard Silly
Born Totnes, Devon, 1846

Susannah Slattern
Baptized Bourne, Lincolnshire, 29 August 1725

R. Slicker
(Male) Died Bradford, Yorkshire, 1876

Charlotte Slob
Baptized St Mary the Virgin, Dover, Kent, 12 July 1805

Nancy Sluggard
Married William Stoneman, Stoke Damerel, Devon, 10 June 1807

Elizabeth Frump Smeath
Married Exeter, Devon, 1841

Susanna Smelly
Baptized Cambusnethan, Lanarkshire 15 September 1695

Inane Barker Smithson
Born Guisborough, Yorkshire, 1879

Samuel Sod
Baptized Bourn, Cambridgeshire, 6 March 1836

William Sodoff
Married Christine Naylor, St Thomas, Dudley, Staffordshire,
3 April 1848

Silly Staryroom
(Female) Born Whissonsett, Norfolk, c.1877
(Hindolveston, Norfolk, 1901 census)

Susannah Rotten Stevens
Married Newton Abbot, Devon, 1876

Melior Strangeman
Baptized Shapwick, Dorset, 2 April 1739

Mary Ann Stupid
Born Middlesex c.1821
(St Dunstan-in-the-West, London, 1841 census)

Feeble Sutcliffe
(Female) Born Erringden, Yorkshire, c.1880 (Erringden, 1881 census)

Richard Pillock Sutton
Born Dover, Kent, 1840

Thomas Tacky
Born Loughborough, Leicestershire, 1860

Kate Terrible
Married Charles Henry Kerry, White Notley, Essex, 16 June 1872

Mary Terror
Born Merthyr Tydfil, Glamorgan, 1856

Laurance [*sic*] Thicky
Born Staines, Middlesex, 1855

Filthy Thiele
Born np c.1879, German subject (Hampstead, London, 1901 census)

Mary Drippy Tilley
Married Spalding, Lincolnshire, 1847

William James Bitch Tolhurst
Born Lambeth, London, 1841

Silly Trollope
(Female) Born Doncaster, Yorkshire, c.1894 (Doncaster, 1901 census)

Thomas Trouble
Married Wincanton, Somerset, 1861

Violet Porteous Twaddle
Born Stonehouse, Lanarkshire, 30 March 1856

Janam Twit
Married Thomas Newton, Wrawby, Lincolnshire, 1606

Frida Mary Ugly
Married Holborn, London, 1907

William Tippen Useless
Baptized Tewkesbury, Gloucestershire, 3 May 1772

Freak Ustick
Buried Egloshayle, Cornwall, 1730

D. Viant
(Male) Born Stoke Damerel, Devon, 1857

E. Vil
(Female) Born Hermitage, Staffordshire, c.1864
(Nottingham, 1881 census)

Oceans Vile
Married Langport, Somerset, 1871

Mamelia Vulgar
Married Dartford, Kent, 1903

Louisa Dippy Walker
Born Hitchin, Hertfordshire, 1841

Ephraim Uriah Weird
Born South Shields, Durham, 1902

James Wells Tawdry Wells
Born Newton Abbot, Devon, 1849

Albenia Whalebelly
Born Rockland St Peter, Norfolk, c.1860 (Griston, Norfolk, 1881 census)

Prickhead Whelan
Born St Helens, Lancashire, c.1858 (Widnes, Lancashire, 1861 census)

Sarah Gobby Whipp
Born Greenwich, Kent, 1856

Elsutt Wicked
Married Roger Crossman, St Maurice, Plympton, Devon, 1663

Drunke Widegans
(Male) Born Romania c.1856
(St George Hanover Square, London, 1891 census)

Dumbo Willans
Born np 1918; died Truro, Cornwall, 2004

Urseley Wimp
Baptized Husthwaite, Yorkshire, 26 June 1755

Mary Jane Hutchcome Wino
Married Plymouth, Devon, 1850

Henry Wuss
Married St Pancras, London, 1902

Phebe Yuck
Baptized Brougham Street Primitive Methodist Chapel, West Hartlepool,
Durham, 20 January 1876

THE ONOMASTIC ORCHESTRA

◆

Hannah Harmonic Barrowcliff
Married Mansfield, Nottinghamshire, 1873

Burt Bass
Married Elizabeth Stapleton, Marston Mortayne, Bedfordshire, 19 May 1757

Andrew White Baton
Baptized Milton, Glasgow, Lanarkshire, 15 September 1873

Isabella Bugle
Baptized Christ Church, Tynemouth,
Northumberland, 18 July 1790

Loudy Cello
Baptized Tywardreath, Cornwall,
2 October 1672

Johannes Cymbal
Baptized St Martin-in-the-Fields,
London, 16 March 1667

Honor Drum
Married Edmond Horele, London,
16 December 1720

Abba Funk
Born St George in the East, London, 1900

John Gong
Baptized St George the Martyr, Southwark,
London, 9 November 1823

Elias Guitar
Married Susanna Jeanmorann, St Dunstan, Stepney, London, 5 October 1713

Harriet Harp
Born Stoke-on-Trent, Staffordshire, 1861

Violet Horn
Born Alloah, Clackmannanshire, 27 October 1863

Johann Sebastian Jagger
Born Whitehaven, Cumberland, 1889

Epiphany Lullaby
Married Veryan, Cornwall, 3 January 1767

Mary Music
Married Joseph Woods, Biggleswade, Bedfordshire, 15 March 1824

Robert Oboe
Married Ann Wigg, Bobbing, Kent, 16 July 1801

Mel Oddy
Born Halifax, Yorkshire, 1886

Oboe Oglesby
(Female) Born Seaham, Durham, c.1899 (Seaham, 1901 census)

Carrie Oke
Born Bideford, Devon, 1864

Lo-Ruhamah Organ
Baptized North Nibley, Gloucestershire, 6 November 1785

Nudina Harriet Organ
Born Cheltenham, Gloucestershire, 1846

Servina Piano
Baptized Escomb, Durham, 31 August 1879

Violin Prigg
(Female) Born Bury St Edmunds, Suffolk, c.1887
(Bury St Edmunds, 1891 census)

Samuel Rapper Scrutton
Married Dewsbury, Yorkshire, 1910

Barbara Seville
Born Birkenhead, Cheshire, c.1882 (Birkenhead, 1901 census)

Topsy Sharp
Born Bristol, Gloucestershire, 1862

Mike Stand
Born Durham c.1844
(Newcastle upon Tyne, Northumberland, 1851 census)

Banjo Thomas
(Male) Born Dudley, Worcestershire, c.1836
(Walsall, Staffordshire, 1871 census)

Tom Tom
Born Bristol, Gloucestershire, c.1862
(Barton Regis, Gloucestershire, 1891 census)

Priscilla Trumpet
Baptized Tipton, Staffordshire, 19 August 1832

John Tuba
Married Sarah Chenery, St Margaret's, Lowestoft, Suffolk, 16 January 1774

I. Tunes
(Female) Married Durham 1874

Roger Viola
Baptized St Mary Whitechapel, Stepney, London, 4 April 1604

Mary Violin
Married John Pearce, St Mary Soho, Westminster, London, 23 August 1870

Concettina [*sic*] Lucia Wilfart
Born np 1928; died Bradford, Yorkshire, 1992

———◆———

TRANSPORTS OF DELIGHT

Submarine Miners Banacks
Born Kingston upon Hull, Yorkshire, c.1837 (Kingston upon Hull, 1891 census)

Mac Maximilian Bike
Born Shoreditch, London, c.1847
(St Mary Aldermanbury, London, 1861 census)

Rhoda Boat
Born Rogate, Hampshire, c.1813 (Graffham, Sussex, 1861 census)

Driver Bus
(Male) Born Somerset c.1879 (Leeds, Yorkshire, 1901 census)

Edward Death Buss
Born Tendring, Essex, 1904

Julia Matilda Trike Cable
Born Stoke Damerel, Devon, 1851

Ford Carr
Born Newcastle upon Tyne, Northumberland, c.1863
(Newcastle upon Tyne, 1871 census)

John Bump Carr
Born Sedgehill, Northumberland, c.1846
(Chirton, Northumberland, 1891 census)

Cycle Cockwell
Born Plymouth, Devon, c.1888 (Plymouth, 1891 census)

Mercedes Conga
Born Brazil c.1856
(Sunnninghill, Berkshire, 1881 census)

Biking Cooper
(Female) Born Wellington, Shropshire, c.1830
(Wellington, 1851 census)

Minnie Cooper
Born Spalding, Lincolnshire, 1859

Leicester Railway Cope
Born Leicester 1864

Bountiful Coupe
Born Bolsover, Derbyshire, 1844

Harley Davidson
Born Cainham, Shropshire c.1879
(Cainham, 1881 census)

Laurie Driver
Born np 1895; died Surrey 1990

Julia Penny Farthing
Born Midhurst, Sussex, 1876

Tranquilline Ferrari
Born Holborn, London, 1895

Zed Flying
Born Portsmouth, Hampshire, c.1884 (West Ham, Essex, 1901 census)

Iva Ford
Born Blything, Suffolk, 1882

Philadelphia Fuel
Baptized Denham, Buckinghamshire, 15 November 1840

Georgiana Top Gear
Born Wambrook, Somerset, c.1862 (Tarrant Hinton, Dorset, 1891 census)

Hy Geers
(Male) Baptized Bridge Sollers, Herefordshire, 26 January 1681

Jane Hardtop
Married John Cheshire, Runcorn, Cheshire, 7 February 1836

Aeronaut Hayes
Born Lincoln c.1865 (Lincoln, 1881 census)

Thomas Tank Hotten
Born Bodmin, Cornwall, 1887

Frederick Petroleum Hughes
Married Islington, London, 1873

Charles Aston Martin
Born St Pancras, London, 1864

Mary Zeppelin Matthewman
Born np 1916; died Rotherham, Yorkshire, 2000

Christ Metro
Born Caithness c.1838 (Wick, Caithness, 1841 Scotland census)

Minnie Minor
Born Bristol, Gloucestershire, 1889

Mary Moped
Born np c.1816 (Barton Regis, Gloucestershire, 1841 census)

Lada Morgan
(Female) Born Colorado, USA, c.1853 (Kensington, London, 1881 census)

Jane Ada Motorhead
Born Great Broughton, Cumberland, c.1874 (Great Broughton, 1881 census)

Messy Parker
(Female) Born Kent c.1839 (Chiddingstone, Kent, 1841 census)

Tram Plant
Married Stourbridge, Worcestershire, 1855

L. Plate
(Female) Born Sussex c.1811 (Warminghurst, Sussex, 1841 census)

Noel Plate
Born Binfield, Buckinghamshire, c.1847 (Hendon, Middlesex, 1891 census)

Brinsley Roy C. Rolls
Born Dorchester, Dorset, 1893

Rover Rolls
Born Cookham, Berkshire, 1891

Sarah Roundabout
Born Sutton, Warwickshire, c.1828 (Kingsbury, Warwickshire, 1851 census)

Phil Rupp
Died Hackney, London, 1856

Hugh Scooter
Married Margaret Kerr, Dalry, Ayrshire, 5 September 1829

John Skoda
Born Glastonbury, Somerset, c.1827 (Evercreech, Somerset, 1871 census)

George Quick Sloman
Died Okehampton, Devon, 1858

Thomas Silly Speed
Born Newark, Nottinghamshire, 1843

Wacke Speed
(Male) Born Bradford, Yorkshire, c.1861 (Bradford, 1881 census)

Anthony Speedo
Married Margaret Barker, Nayland, Suffolk, 25 October 1562

Mary Petrol Swanson
Born Bridgend, Glamorgan, 1901

John Turbo Tapper
Married Birmingham, Warwickshire, 1879

Pilot Tidd
Died Houghton-le-Spring, Durham, 1882

William Tooslow
Baptized Topsham, Devon, 6 April 1652

Funily Tram
Born Newcastle upon Tyne, Northumberland, c.1848
(Newcastle upon Tyne, 1881 census)

Minnie Wheels
Born Chelsea, London, c.1857 (Bermondsey, London, 1881 census)

Gasoline McKenzie Yeats
Born Manchester, Lancashire, 1845

———◆———

OUT OF THE CLOSET

Nellie Knickerbocker Beach
Married Paddington, London, 1907

Freeston Blazer
(Female) Married Thomas James, West Bradenham, Norfolk, 6 December 1756

Sarah Bloomers
Baptized St Leonard, New Malton, Yorkshire, 1 March 1792

Jack Boot
Born Uxbridge, Middlesex, 1899

Wellington Boot
Born Linton, Cambridgeshire, 1869

Cashmere Boss
Born Louth, Lincolnshire, 1849

Thomas Bowtie
Married Agnes Myller, St Andrew,
Plymouth, Devon, 25 January 1613

John Bra
Born Hardwick, Devon, c.1851
('draper's assistant',
City of London, 1881 census)

Sarah Braces
Born Wandsworth, London, 1841

Pinkus Brief
Born Whitechapel, London, 1911

Zipper Brotherwood
Born Uckfield, Sussex, 1885

William Brownhat
Married Elizabeth Jordan, St John the Baptist,
Croydon, Surrey, 7 September 1813

Lively Busby
(Male) Born np c.1832; died Chertsey, Surrey, 1907

Pearl Button
Born Hollingbourne, Kent, 1903

Fanny Cap
Married Charles Panton, Hemingbrough, Yorkshire, 7 September 1876

Sophia Clothes
Born Ashton-under-Lyne, Lancashire, 1843

Panty Coppola
Married Rose Johnson, St Pancras, London, 1918

Agnea Corset
Born Ulverston, Lancashire, 1875

and

Agnea Winship Corset
Born Tynemouth, Northumberland, 1875

*Only two Agnea Corsets are recorded, both of them
born in the same year.*

Lapel Davies
(Female) Born Lambeth, London, c.1890
(St George the Martyr, London, 1891 census)

Polly Esther
Born Bradford, Yorkshire, c.1870 (Manningham, Yorkshire, 1871 census)

Maggie Shirt Fidler
Born Chapel-en-le-Frith, Derbyshire, 1897

Mary Gestring
Born Shropshire c.1830 (Shifnal, Shropshire, 1841 census)

Brown Hatt
Born Bury, Lancashire, c.1842 (Musbury, Lancashire, 1871 census)

Topsy Hatter
Born Rye, East Sussex, 1898

Jean Jacket
Born Ireland c.1837 (Paisley, Renfrewshire, 1841 Scotland census)

Levi Jeans
Baptized Stalbridge, Dorset, 24 February 1811

Charles Knicker
Married Ann Coradine, St Michael, Tatenhill, Staffordshire, 13 April 1700

Flares Moore
(Female) Born Birmingham, Warwickshire, c.1856
(Handsworth, Staffordshire, 1871 census)

Elizabeth Nylon
Died Lambeth, London, 1853

Jemima Panties
Born Poplar, London, c.1846 (Poplar, 1861 census)

Elizabeth Pantoff
Married William Hutt, St Botolph without Bishopsgate, London,
17 September 1751

Mary Panty
Baptized Glatton, Huntingdonshire, 1 September 1751

George Clap Plimsoll
Married Bristol, Gloucestershire, 1875

Anna Rack
Married St George in the East, London, 1881

T. Shirt
(Male) Born Ecclesfield, Yorkshire, 1843

Jim Shoe
Married Bawdrip, Somerset, 28 February 1602

Sadie Shorts
Born West Derby, Lancashire, 1901

Minnie Skirt
Baptized St Mary's, Sandwich, Kent, 17 July 1777

Mary Bra Small
Born Newcastle, Northumberland, c.1861
(Westgate, Northumberland, 1861 census)

Elizabeth Snickers
Married Robert Musgrave, Burneston, Yorkshire, 20 December 1751

Emmaretta Snood
Married Lexden, Essex, 1881

Martha Socks
Married John Truman, Stapleford, Nottinghamshire, 27 June 1762

Archibald Sporran
Born Cambeltown, Argyll, 21 January 1855

Nanny G. String
Born Gateshead, Durham, c.1859 (Gateshead, 1861 census)

Ana Sweater
Married Michael Pollard, Halifax, Yorkshire, 18 July 1670

Original Walker John Bedford Thong
Died Huntingdon 1858

Maud Camelia Tights
Born Cambridge 1876

Florenett Trousers
(Female) Born np c.1852, Walsall, Staffordshire
(Paddington, London, 1881 census)

Violet Trunks
Born Williton, Somerset, 1898

Rebecca Vest
Born Ludlow, Shropshire, 1844

Frock Watton
Born Solihull, Warwickshire, 1860

Trainers Wheatfield
(Male) Born St Luke, London, c.1850 (St Luke, 1861 census)

Felty Wooley
(Female) Born Radford, Nottinghamshire, c.1889
(Bulwell, Nottinghamshire, 1891 census)

Glad Wragg
Born Bakewell, Derbyshire, 1894

Collar Zacks
Born Riga, Russia, c.1870 (St George in the East, London, 1891 census)

Matthias Zip
Baptized Heworth, Durham, 23 September 1705

GOOD SPORTS

◆

Batty Ball
(Female) Born North Meols, Lancashire, c.1797 (North Meols, 1871 census)

Mary Bowley Ball
Born USA c.1850 (Loughborough, Leicestershire, 1891 census)

Spinner Ball
Born Wanstead, Essex, c.1900 (Wanstead, 1901 census)

Mark Foot Balls
Born South Shields, Durham, 1890

Olympic Bell
Born Lanchester, Durham, 1889

Tom Bola
Born Sheffield, Yorkshire, c.1841 (Sheffield, 1851 census)

Tennis Bust
Born Stonebroom, Derbyshire, c.1897 (Shirland, Derbyshire, 1901 census)

Bartholemew Cricket
Baptized St John, Margate, Kent, 25 April 1755

Cricket Crisp
(Female) Born Bath, Somerset, c.1838
(Walcot, Somerset, 1851 census)

Francois Croquet
Baptized French Huguenot Church,
Threadneedle Street, London,
28 November 1744

Dan Darts
Born Biggleswade, Bedfordshire, 1874

Sarah Bounce P. Frisby
Born Leicester 1878

Fanny Golf
Married George Rolph,
Cardiff, Glamorgan, 1915

Sarah Googly
Married Henry Cork, St John the Evangelist,
Limehouse, London, 9 August 1859

Sporty Gray
Born Alton, Hampshire, 1897

Hannah Hurdles
Born Reading, Berkshire, 1883

Frisby Lightfoot
Born Luton, Bedfordshire, 1873

Jim Locker
Married Stoke-on-Trent, Staffordshire, 1864

Marathon Beatrice Pearson
Born Warwick 1889

Jack Potts
Born Wolstanton, Staffordshire, 1902

Wrestle Raynsford
Born Guildford, Surrey, 1873

Thomas Rodeo
Baptized St Margaret's, Durham, 17 April 1808

Lavinia Roulette
Married Lambeth, London, 1859

C. Saw
(Male) Born Edmonton, Middlesex, 1879

William Snooker
Married Ann Kerwood, Bosham, Sussex, 25 September 1775

Gladys Badminton Sweett
Born Devonport, Devon, 1903

Thomas Tenpin
Born Plymouth, Devon, c.1837 (Rattery, Devon, 1901 census)

Lot Terry
Born Prestwich, Lancashire, 1884

Rugby Thrower
Died King's Lynn, Norfolk, 1895

Urban Wicket
Born Sheviock, Cornwall, c.1633

Uncommon Smiths

The most recent estimate of the number of people in England and Wales with the surname 'Smith' was 652,563. And forget all those 'Mcs' – Smith is by a long margin the most common surname in Scotland as well. About twelve people out of every thousand in the UK are called Smith. In the period 1837–2005, 53,350 babies were given the archetypal name 'John Smith', and there are 12,793 of them currently on the National Health Service Register. If you happen to be called Smith there is therefore a clear temptation to elevate your child above the commonplace by coming up with a first name that is a little different.

Abishag Martha Smith
Born Thraptson, Northamptonshire, 1876

Amorous Smith
Born Bury, Lancashire, 1858

Anonymous Smith
Married Eleanor Carlisle, Leckhampton, Buckinghamshire, 17 May 1604

Blondina Smith
Born np c.1826; died Hemel Hempstead, Hertfordshire, 1893

Bonus Smith
Born Skipton, Yorkshire, 1843

Brick Smith
Died York 1851

Cleopatra Smith
Born Newington, London, 1860

Cock Smith
Born Yorkshire c.1839 (Kirk Burton, Yorkshire, 1841 census)

Cockshott Smith Smith
Born Keighley, Yorkshire, 1845

Cuckoo Smith
Born Brimpton, Berkshire, c.1877 (Brimpton, 1881 census)

Cupid Aaron T. Smith
Born Wandsworth, London, 1870

Despair Smith
Born Ely, Cambridgeshire, 1856

Devil Smith
(Female) Born np c.1816 (St Pancras, London, 1841 census)

Dorothy Rubbery Smith
Born West Bromwich, Staffordshire, 1900

Dozer Smith
Born Kettering Northamptonshire, 1893

Dripper Smith
(Female) Born Whaplode, Lincolnshire, c.1882 (Whaplode, 1901 census)

Elizabeth Utterly Smith
Married Glanford Brigg, Lincolnshire, 1865

Elsie Penile Smith
Died Barton Regis, Gloucestershire, 1894

Exuperius Smith
(Male) Baptized Whitford, Flintshire, 18 October 1818

Fang Smith
(Female) Born Hopesay, Shropshire, c.1848
(Woolston, Shropshire, 1851 census)

Fortunate Hortensius Smith
Married Reading, Berkshire, 1884

Frank Walrus Smith
Born Portsea Island, Hampshire, 1880

George Wackerbarth Smith
Born Wirral, Cheshire, 1851

Gladys Passion Smith
Born Bristol, Gloucestershire, 1904

Goliath Smith
Born Buckingham 1844

Goon Smith
Born Surrey c.1854 (London, 1871 census)

Hairy Smith
Born Keighley, Yorkshire, c.1877 (Keighley, 1881 census)

Hannah Booby Smith
Born Cirencester, Gloucestershire, 1842

Hannibal Smith
Born Houghton-le-Spring, Durham, 1862

Harry Two Smith
Married Derby, Derbyshire, 1900

Henry Waste Smith
Born Nuneaton, Warwickshire, 1901

Hiawatha Smith
Born Islington, London, 1890

Indiana Smith
Born Colchester, Essex, 1852

Jesus Smith
Born Angus c.1823 (Brechin, Angus, 1841 census)

John Philosopher Smith
Born Aston, Warwickshire, 1879

Julius Caesar Smith
Born Leverington, Cambridgeshire, c.1821
(Kirton, Lincolnshire, 1851 census)

Kaiser Smith
Born Warwick 1873

Lewis Unexpected Smith
Born Medway, Kent, 1899

Lichen M. J. Smith
(Female) Born Birmingham c.1848 (Aston, Warwickshire, 1871 census)

Lizzie Muffin Smith
Born Burton upon Trent, Staffordshire, 1898

Lustrous Luke Smith
Married Ipswich, Suffolk, 1858

Mango Smith
(Male) Born Scotland c.1804 (Litchurch, Derbyshire, 1871 census)

Maudlin Smith
Born Durham 1864

Messiah Smith
Born Sheffield, Yorkshire, 1848

Mice Smith
(Female) Born Cradley, Herefordshire, c.1867
(Suckley, Worcestershire, 1871 census)

Minge Smith
Born Crich, Derbyshire, c.1860 (Holbeck, Nottinghamshire, 1891 census)

Minniehaha Smith
Born Gravesend, Kent, nd (Gravesend, 1881 census)

Murder John Smith
Born St George Hanover Square, London, 1878

Mystic Smith
Born South Stoneham, Hampshire, 1855

Nebuchadnezzar Smith
Born Hollingbourne, Kent, 1882

Perpugilliam Smith
Born West Bromwich, Staffordshire, 1847

Perseverance Smith
Born Fulham, London, 1876

Pickles Smith
Born Burnley, Lancashire, 1863

Plato Smith
Born Blything, Suffolk, 1880

Ponce Smith
(Male) Born Hellington, Shropshire, c.1833
(Chorlton-cum-Hardy, Lancashire, 1891 census)

President Percy Smith
Born Poplar, London, 1882

Queen Victoria Smith
Born Rochford, Essex, 1901

Rap Smith
Born Doncaster, Yorkshire, 1900

Semen Smith
Born Burrough on the Hill, Leicestershire, c.1834
(Burton upon Trent, Staffordshire, 1861 census)

Sexey Jane Smith
Born np c.1842; died Amesbury, Wiltshire, 1898

Shed Smith
Born Hoxne, Yorkshire, 1885

Speedy Smith
(Female) Born St Helens, Lancashire, c.1885
(Lockwood, Yorkshire, 1891 census)

Streaker Smith
(Male) Born Easington, Durham, 1845

Submit Smith
(Female) Born Hatfield, Hertfordshire, c.1736

Suckey Smith
(Female) Born Gloucestershire c.1868
(Little Rissington, Gloucestershire, 1881 census)

Susannah Ink Smith
Married Manchester, Lancashire, 1863

Tilgathpilneser Smith
Born Newmarket, Suffolk, 1861
*After Mahershalalhashbaz, Tilgathpilneser is one of the
longest personal names in the Bible.*

Tin Smith
Born np c.1876; died Sleaford, Lincolnshire, 1884

Uz Smith
Born Hoxne, Yorkshire, 1892

Vaulter Smith
(Male) Born Thurne, Norfolk, c.1855 (Thurne, 1861 census)

Warp Smith
(Male) Born Manchester, Lancashire, c.1846 Manchester, 1891 census)

William Whynot Smith
Born Ipswich, Suffolk, 1861

Wonderful Smith
Born Blything, Suffolk, 1893

REVERSE NAMES

◆

These are names where placing the surname first (in the form Smith, John) changes the meaning, sometimes making the innocuous noxious...

Charlotte Apple
Born Germany c.1847 (Kingston upon Hull, Yorkshire, 1851 census)

Fanny Bare
Baptized Milton Damerel, Devon, 31 December 1826

Willy Big
Married Rachel Haselwood, Dartford, Kent, 5 October 1626

William Job Blow
Born Lincoln 1887

Dick Chew
Born np 1912; died Blackburn, Lancashire, 2003

Comfort Close
Born Ross, Herefordshire, 1869

Feel Copper
Born Rochdale, Lancashire, 1850 (Rochdale, 1851 census)

Fanny Damp
Born Chard, Devon, 1844

Kate Forni
Born Austria c.1865 (St Martin-in-the-Fields, London, 1891, census)

Dick Hard
Baptized Alford, Lincolnshire, 24 August 1652

Dick Huge
Born Wales c.1865 (Marsden, Yorkshire, 1891 census)

Fanny Huge
Born Kenwyn, Cornwall, c.1807 (Kenwyn, 1851 census)

Roger Jolly
Baptized Parham, Suffolk, 15 April 1549

Dick Longest
Baptized Bletchworth, Surrey, 18 July 1602

Christmas Merry
Born Williton, Somerset, 1885

Dick Moby
Born Woodstock, Oxfordshire, 1876

Fanny Moist
Born Newton Abbot, Devon, 1850

Dick Nice
Baptized All Saints, Sudbury, Suffolk, 31 July 1778

Fanny Nice
Born Sheffield, Yorkshire, 1904

Dick Pink
Baptized Hambledon, Hampshire, 20 August 1647

Fanny Pink
Born Malling, Kent, 1853

Jane Plain
Married John Rogers, Shernborne, Norfolk, 11 October 1757

Crusoe Robinson
Born Wortley, Yorkshire, 1888

Fanny Shaves
Born Doncaster, Yorkshire, c.1860 (Doncaster, 1871 census)

Billy Silly
Baptized Markfield, Leicestershire, 13 September 1603

Dick Slippery
Married Anne Gipson, St Dunstan, Stepney, London, 21 December 1675

Argument Small
Born Guisborough, Yorkshire, 1853

Dick Stiff
Born St Luke, London, 1846

Fanny Tight
Born Ware, Hertfordshire, 1847

Christmas White
Born Boston, Lincolnshire, 1858

Enough Wright
(Male) Born Shropshire c.1835 (Wellington, Shropshire, 1841 census)

BEST SPOONERISM NAMES

◆

Joe Blobs
Married Sarah Smith, Sedgley, Staffordshire, 11 September 1803

Fanny Cucker
Born Sutton, Surrey, c.1857 (Sutton, 1871 census)

Harry Punt Cunnington
Born Lutterworth, Leicestershire, 1875

Mary Hinge
Born Clutton, Somerset, 1846

Carrie Hunt
Born Havant, Hampshire, 1879

Kenny Lunt
Born West Derby, Lancashire, 1910

Betty Swall
Married Auckland, Durham, 1860

RHYMES WITHOUT REASON

◆

Mabel Abel
Born Norwich, Norfolk, c.1895 (Norwich 1901 census)

Sally Alley
Born Yorkshire c.1825 (Halifax, Yorkshire, 1841 census)

Paul Ball
Baptized Bath Abbey, Somerset, 7 February 1599

Anna Banner
Born Liverpool, Lancashire, 1879

Charley Barley
Born New Cross, Kent, c.1857 (Croydon, Surrey, 1861 census)

Harry Barry
Born Frome, Somerset, 1842

Peter Beater
Baptized West Teignmouth, Devon, 17 August 1809

Ethel Bethel
Born Stockport, Cheshire, 1905

Ruth Booth
Baptized St Bartholemew Exchange, London, 18 June 1580

John Nooks Brooks
Married Lambeth, London, 1862

Lizzie Busy
Baptized Modbury, Devon, 18 July 1632

Mary Canary
Born Prescot, Lancashire, 1859

Harry Carry
Born Folkestone, Kent, c.1901 (Folkestone, 1901 census)

Agnise Chemise
Married Alexander Biggar, Canongate,
Edinburgh, Midlothian, 27 October 1566

Hester Chester
Born Blackburn, Lancashire, 1862

Nancy Clancy
Born Brent, Devon, c.1847 (Brent, 1871 census)

Mary Dairy
Married John Homes, Whitgift, Yorkshire, 10 January 1809

Sam Dam
Born Stoke Prior, Herefordshire, c.1795
(Kingsland, Herefordshire, 1851 census)

Andy Dandy
Baptized St Stephen Walbrook, London, 28 May 1712

Mark Dark
Born Keynsham, Somerset, 1867

Cow Dow
Married Grantham, Lincolnshire, 1858

Peter Eater
Born Cheshire c.1781 (Great Budworth, Cheshire, 1841 census)

Mary Fairy
Baptized Ringstead, Northamptonshire, 16 June 1763

Nancy Fancy
Born np 1928; died Surrey 2001

Danny Fanny
Born Rotherfield, Sussex, c.1834 (Hamsey, Sussex, 1871 census)

Richard Stoat Float
Born Devon c.1821 (East Stonehouse, Devon, 1851 census)

Caroline Toil Foil
Born Sidbury, Devon, c.1816 (Honiton, Devon, 1861 census)

Maude Ford
Born Yeovil, Somerset, 1862

Sand Gand
(Female) Born Kingsbridge, Devon, c.1807 (Chatham, Kent, 1881 census)

Sander Gander
(Female) Born Middlesex c.1774 (St Mary Whitechapel, London, 1841 census)

Sandy Gandy
Married John Evans, Davenham, Cheshire, 31 October 1814

Hugh Glue
Married Ann White, Chelsea, London, 1804

Norman Gorman
Born Pendleton, Lancashire, c.1884 (Pendleton, 1891 census)

Mary Hairy
Married Helmsley, Yorkshire, 1861

Fred Head
Born Stockbridge, Hampshire, 1865

Rose Hose
Born Retford, Nottinghamshire, c.1871
(Laneham, Nottinghamshire, 1871 census)

Molly Jolly
Born np 1912; died Oxford 1991

Sidney Kidney
Born Milton, Kent, 1906

Amy Lamy
Born USA c.1866 (St Saviour, Jersey, 1891 Channel Islands census)

Peg Legg
Born Stuntney, Cambridgeshire, c.1900 (Ely, Cambridgeshire, 1901 census)

Hugh Loo
Died South Shields, Durham, 1878

Ronald McDonald
Married Agnes Cameron, Dunblane, Perthshire, 20 April 1689

Thigh McKay
Born Scotland c.1806 (Brighthelmston (Brighton), 1841 census)

Peter Meter
Born Aberdeenshire c.1821 (Aberdeen, 1841 Scotland census)

June Moon
Born Bedfordshire c.1801 (Bedford, 1841 census)

William Organ Morgan
Born Medway, Kent, 1858

Eater Neater
Born Islington, London, c.1835 (Dulwich, London, 1871 census)

Willy Nilly
Married Johan [sic] Crosman, Plympton St Mary, Devon, 26 September 1648

Enoch Nock
Born Wolverhampton, Staffordshire, 1841

Percy Nursey
Born Lambeth, London, 1871

Jane Pain
Baptized Perranzabuloe, Cornwall, 29 October 1682

Hatty Patty
Born Chelsea, London, c.1830 (Islington, London, 1851 census)

Henny Penny
(Male) Born Llanasa, Flintshire, Wales c.1839 (Llanasa, 1901 Wales census)

Berry Perry
(Female) Born Fowey, Cornwall, c.1851 (Fowey, 1871 census)

Louisa Pizza
Born Blything, Suffolk, 1839

Dick Prick
Baptized Barrow, Suffolk, 1 July 1544

Hugh Pugh
Born Llanfihangel-y-Pennant, Merionethshire, 24 February 1826

Ice Rice
(Male) Born St Pancras, London, c.1860 (St Pancras, 1861 census)

Mary Scary
Born Docking, Norfolk, 1843

Herbert Sherbert
Born Tottenham, London, c.1880 (Stoke Newington, London, 1891 census)

Dick Sick
Married Margaret Bennett, Kirkham, Lancashire, 1 February 1562

Nellie Smellie
Born St Pancras, London, 1897

John Long Song
Born Oldham, Lancashire, c.1825 (Whitley, Derbyshire, 1871 census)

I. Spy
(Male) Born Tillicoultry, Clackmannanshire, c.1805
(Row, Dumbarton, 1861 Scotland census)

Ray Spray
Born Sussex c.1895 (Lewisham, London, 1901 census)

Jack Tack
Born Portsmouth, Hampshire, 1906

Rash Tash
Born Germany c.1871 (St Mary Whitechapel, London, 1871 census)

Jane Vane
Baptized Stanhope, Durham, 29 August 1653

Dick Vick
Born Alverstoke, Hampshire, 1843

Jim Vim
Born Sussex c.1824 (Brighthelmston (Brighton), Sussex, 1841 census)

Sam Yam
Born Leeds, Yorkshire, 1900

HORRIFIC HONORIFICS

◆

Although these sound like a titled lot, their grandiloquent first names are those with which they were born.

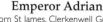

Emperor Adrian
Born St James, Clerkenwell Green,
London, 7 May 1809

Reverend James Ball
Born Doncaster, Yorkshire, 1878

Lord Baron
Born Haslingden, Lancashire, 1842

Marquis Baron
Born Burnley, Lancashire, 1880

Saint Bugg
Died Bourne, Lincolnshire, 1840

King Solomon Coe
Born Caxton, Cambridgeshire, 1893

William The Second Davy
Born Romford, Essex, 1890

Duke Dyke
Born St Thomas, Devon, 1849

Sir Dusty Entwistle
Born Bury, Lancashire, c.1877 (Bury, 1881 census)

Bishop Fanny
Born Lutterworth, Leicestershire, 1844

Doctor Septimus Forrest
Born Preston, Lancashire, c.1834 (Blackburn, Lancashire, 1851 census)
*Seventh sons were believed to possess special powers, and were
sometimes given the name 'Doctor', especially in Lancashire.*

King George
Baptized St Martin-in-the-Fields, London, 27 May 1724

Princess Gladys Glastonbury
Born Keynsham, Somerset, 1902

Viscount Heavican
Born Bury, Lancashire, 1890 (Bury, 1891 census)

Surgeon Kershaw
Born Basford, Nottinghamshire, 1860

Czarina Podmore
Born Burslem, Staffordshire, c.1842 (Burslem, 1891 census)

Queen Prince
Died Chester, Cheshire, 1894

Marquis Marquis F. Puschart
Married St Saviour, London, 1892

Sirjohn Robinson
Baptized Old Church, St Pancras, London, 22 March 1796

Pope Smyrk
Married Brighton, East Sussex, 1907

Baron Tool
Married Scarborough, Yorkshire, 1855

Percy King Tutt
Born Highworth, Wiltshire, 1893
*He was not named after King Tutankhamun, whose tomb
was not discovered until 1922.*

Queen Victoria
Born np c.1840 (Edmonton, Middlesex, 1851 census)

General Washington
Born Halifax, Yorkshire, 1842

Prince Charles Whales
Born Mitford, Norfolk, 1899

King Wong
Married Liverpool, Lancashire, 1934
The film King Kong *had been released the previous year.*

Cardinal Woolsey
Born Croydon, Surrey, 1844

Lady Godiva A. Wright
Born Brixton, Devon, c.1849 (Plymouth, Devon, 1891 census)

THE HUMAN GAZETTEER

◆

Percy Stonehenge W. Ansell
Born St Olave, Southwark, London, 1874

Albania Ash
Born Penzance, Cornwall, 1900

Ann Gibraltar Billing
Born Liverpool, Lancashire, 1846

Armenia Binks
Born Westminster, London, 1869

Henry Barbados Bright
Married Lambeth, London, 1846

Argentina Bull
Born St Pancras, London, 1876

Tunis Butterfly
Baptized Wombourn, Staffordshire, 25 June 1686

Windsor Castle
Born Radford, Nottinghamshire, 1876

William Himalaya Chapman
Born Birmingham, Warwickshire, 1888

Burma Christmas
(Female) Born Hounslow, Middlesex, c.1843 (Brighton, Sussex, 1871 census)

Siberia Constable
Born Swansea, Glamorgan, 1838

Anglo America Craven
Born Keighley, Yorkshire, 1852

Phila Delphia
Born Cornwall 1840 (Buryan, Penwith, Cornwall, 1841 census)

Sarah Desert
Baptized St Leonard, Shoreditch, London, 1 April 1804

Tiny England
Born Chorlton, Lancashire, 1888
Not to be confused with Little Britain.

May Fair
Born Nantwich, Cheshire, 1880
The cockney pronunciation of 'Mayfair', the smart area of London,
gave rise to the title of the musical My Fair Lady.

Florida Fleetwood
Baptized Barkway, Hertfordshire, 1 November 1597

Robert Scunthorpe Free
Born Wisbech, Cambridgeshire, 1906

Arctic Franklin Gray
Born Barton-upon-Irwell, Lancashire, 1891
His name commemorates British Arctic explorer John Franklin,
whose expedition was trapped in ice and perished in 1847.

Atlas Hilton
(Male) Born Oldham, Lancashire, 1875

Australia Hilton
Married Barton-upon-Irwell, Lancashire, 1850

Ida Hoe
Born Chorlton, Lancashire, 1878

Phillip Ines
Born np c.1821 (St Paul, Covent Garden, London, 1841 census)

River Jordan
Born Stoke-on-Trent, Staffordshire, 1860

Dover Mongolia R. T. Jose
Born Redruth, Cornwall, 1903

Edwin Singapore Keen
Married East Stonehouse, Devon, 1889

Mary Land
Baptized Taynton, Gloucestershire, 2 February 1599

Luther Denmark Longbottom
(Male) Born Silsden, Yorkshire, c.1848 (Silsden, 1881 census)

Iris Korea Ludlow
Born Dartford, Kent, 1904

Flushing Meadows
(Male) Born Shoreditch, London, 1878

Handel Moscow
Born Wakefield, Yorkshire, c.1857
(Sandal Magna, Yorkshire, 1901 census)

Inconstant Hastings Ogle
Born Newcastle upon Tyne, Northumberland, 1852

Cold Pacific
(Female) Born Middlesex c.1832 (Bow, London, 1881 census)

Tasmania Palfrey
Married Newport, Monmouthshire, 1882

Hyde Park
Died Kensington, London, 1864

Iceland Parrott
Born North Aylesford, Kent, 1872

Robert Hong Kong Phillips
Died Medway, Kent, 1846

Philadelphia Plenty
Baptized St Sepulchre, London, 11 May 1819

William Brazil Pratt
Born St Marylebone, London, 1847

Sweden Rich
(Male) Married Holborn, London, 1845

Lebanon Senior
Born Pontefract, Yorkshire, 1862

Indiana Sevil
Married Sherborne, Dorset, 1853

Minnie Sowter
Born Mansfield, Nottinghamshire, 1893

Ethiopia Maud Stemp
Born Guildford, Surrey, 1871

Tennie C. Street
(Female) Born Hampshire c.1894 (Bournemouth, Hampshire, 1901 census)

Windermere Bigot Stringwell
Born np c.1854; died Chorlton, Lancashire, 1881

Germany Swan
Married Whitechapel, London, 1888

Curly Tennessee
Born Shalford, Essex, c.1887 (West Ham, Essex, 1891 census)

James Afghanistan Tomblin
Born Leigh, Lancashire, 1880

Nan Tucket
Baptized Upton Pyne, Devon, 21 November 1790

Venice Waters
Married Barnet, Hertfordshire, 1850

Holly Wood
Born Faversham, Kent, 1901

A BOY NAMED SUE

Although relatively rare, there are a number of examples of children who, for one reason or another (often the obsequiousness of a parent), ended with a transgender name.

Male

Queen Arthur
Born Dumfries, c.1861
(Preston, Lancashire, 1891 census)

Deborah Brown
Son of Richard and Rebecca Brown,
born Worcestershire, c.1889
(Brierley Hill, Staffordshire, 1891 census)

Fanny Duckhouse
Son of Samuel Duckhouse, born Bloxwich, Staffordshire
c.1896 (Wolverhampton, 1901 census)

Lord Anne Hamilton
Son of the 4th Duke of Hamilton, born 12 October 1709
Anne was named after his godmother, Queen Anne.

Caroline Robert Herbert
Son of Thomas Herbert, 8th Earl of Pembroke, born 28 September 1751
Caroline was the godson of Queen Caroline.

Sir Frederick Anne Hervey
Born np 18 June 1783; died 20 September 1824

Sue Yates
Son of Thomas Yates, born Huddersfield, Yorkshire, c.1847
(Salford, Lancashire, 1871 census)

Female

Nigel E. Bebb
Daughter of Ann Bebb, born Little Hereford, Herefordshire, c.1897
(Little Hereford, 1901 census)

Dorothy Tony Blair
Born Altrincham, Cheshire, 1889

Noah Brittain
Daughter of Albert and Emely [sic] Brittain,
born Patricroft, Lancashire, c.1895 (Eccles, 1901 census)
*A female Noah has biblical authority: Noah was one of the
daughters of Zelophehad,* Numbers 36:11.

Jude Dustman
Married Michael Fox, Old Church, St Pancras, London, 29 September 1828

Reginald Partridge
Born Odell, Bedfordshire, c.1885 (Odell, 1891 census)

Frederick Ann Payne
Daughter of Thomas and Mary Ann Payne, born Liverpool, Lancashire, c.1856
(West Derby, Lancashire, 1871 census)

Douglas Sheffield
Daughter of Sir John Sheffield, born Milgrave, Lincolnshire c.1612

Philip Speke
Daughter of George Speke, born np c.1663

Percy Steak
Married Michael Warrant, St Nicholas, Great Yarmouth,
Norfolk, 23 February 1796

Lawrence Anna Yawn
Born Chertsey, Surrey, 1901 (Chertsey, 1901 census)

MADE FOR EACH OTHER

◆

Just as the phenomenon of nominative determinism seems to compel people to work in professions appropriate to their names, so there is a kind of marital determinism that leads people with apt (or otherwise) surnames to end up together:

Aston–Martin

Karen N. Aston married Jonathan R. Martin, York, 1997
One of six Aston–Martin marriages in the period 1987–2002.

Bell–Bottoms

William S. Bell married Barbara A. Bottoms, Chester-le-Street, Durham, 1912

Cannon–Ball

Ann Cannon married John Ball, St Saviour, Southwark, London, 1830

Cock–Roach

Hannah Cock married Thomas Roach, Burnley, Yorkshire, 1912

Flower–Power

Carl E. V. Flower married Rebecca B. J. Power, Dudley, West Midlands, 1996

Fucks–Allott

George Fucks married Alice Allott, Thurmaston, Leicestershire, 1764

Hard–Cocks

Keith A. Hard married Jennifer A. Cocks, Surrey, 1989

Holmes–Watson

Abraham Holmes married Mary E. Watson, Keighley, Yorkshire, 1915
One of seven Holmes–Watson marriages 1912–15.

King–Kong

Jeremy B. King married Rosalyn L. Kong, Sodbury, Gloucestershire, 1989

Needle–Cotton

Gary J. W. Needle married Samantha L. Cotton, Rochdale, Lancashire, 2002

Quick–Lay

Paul R. Quick married Sara E. Lay, Cambridge, 1989

Wang–King

Yuan Y. Wang married John G. King, Kensington & Chelsea, London, 1997

TECHNO BABEL

◆

Windows Aldridge
Born Staines, Middlesex, c.1848 (Staines, 1861 census)

Elizabeth Backup
Married South Leith, Midlothian, 11 November 1708

Sarah Blog Baker
Married East Stonehouse, Devon, 1839

James Fax Bee
Born Fosdyke Fen, Lincolnshire, c.1835 (Boston, Lincolnshire, 1851 census)

Samson Blog
Born Whitechapel, London, 1893

William Broadband
Baptized South Leith, Midlothian, 4 October 1660

Elizabeth Byte
Married Robert Whittle, Standish, Lancashire, 1 August 1586

Mary Cordless
Born np c.1817; died Manchester, Lancashire, 1874

Telegraph Dick
Born np c.1844; died Bishop Auckland, Durham, 1877

Mary Ann Elizabeth Diskette
Born Plymouth, Devon, 1837

Nancy M. S. Dos
Born np 1914; died South Warwickshire, 2001

Temperantia Google
Baptized Aldborough, Norfolk, 13 August 1598

William Hardisk
Died Knaresborough, Yorkshire, 1851

E. Mail
Born Malmesbury, Wiltshire, 1855

Ann Mobile
Baptized Deddington, Oxfordshire, 21 March 1730

Priscilla Monitor
Died St Marylebone, London, 1840

Ann Ode
Born West Derby, Lancashire, 1846

Cath Ode
Born Wigan, Lancashire, 1898

Lincoln Phone
Baptized Melksham, Wiltshire, 18 February 1803

Elizabeth Pixel
Married William Harford, Kinver, Staffordshire, 19 July 1695

I. Pod
(Male) Baptized Whatfield, Suffolk, 20 May 1638

Philip Radar
Born Stepney, London, 1888

Anna Robot
Born Germany c.1821 (St George Hanover Square, London, 1851 census)
The word 'robot' was invented by Czech writer Karel Capek in
his play R.U.R. (Rossum's Universal Robots) (1920), which
was translated into English in 1928.

Marmaduke Router
Married Elizabeth Worborn, Copgrove, Yorkshire, 26 November 1723

Alys Skype
Baptized St James Garlickhythe, London, 15 May 1560

William Spam
Baptized St Bride's Fleet Street, London, 10 June 1607

Minnie Satellite Spry
Born Sheppey, Kent, 1883

Thomas Text
Born Bourne, Lincolnshire, 1887

Video Thompson
(Female) Born Montevideo, Uruguay, c.1872
(Liverpool, Lancashire, 1881 census)

T. Vee
(Male) Born Boston, Lincolnshire, c.1804
(Skirbeck, Lincolnshire, 1851 census)

Thomas Quark Vernon
Born West Derby, Lancashire, 1901

Chapter Nine

THE SAGA

CONTINUES

The following is a selection of unusual surnames and given names recorded in birth, marriage and death registers in recent years. As with the preceding entries, they are all true, but details have been omitted to preserve their anonymity – though how anonymous can you be if you are called Lollipop or Frisbee?

Tina Ager

X. Rae Alberts

Desiree Skylark Alder

Nonita B. Aspirin

Chris P. Bacon

Jenna Crystal Ball

Leanne Crystal J. Ball

Betty Bangs

Anita Bath

Unique Keanu S. Bee

Luxury Lupin Bell

Eva Bendova

Mercedes Bent

Mercedes Bentley

Anal M. Bile

Tick H. Bong

Amelia Delicious Bosomworth

Emily Jordan Bosomworth

Jedidah A. Breakfast

Calamity Therese Brent

Koala E. Broadfoot

Chromium Brown

Harry Fabulous Brown

Perry Alpachino Brown

Aaron Lamborghini M. Burris

Anus Asif Butt

Barry Cade

Justine Case

Sphinx Charnley

Bamboo Cheeseman

Francesca Coconut Coby

Phlegon J. Cocksedge

Hobbit J. Coward

Ebenezer Hedgehog T. Cringebottom

Icicle Star Crumplin

Possible Dadson Dadson

Savannah Marijuana S. Daly

Ann D'Anna

Katrina Demeanour

Ben Photon Denton

Attila F. Dervish

Anita Dick

Cairo Devontae A. Digital

Su Doku

Lynne C. Doyle

Sundance Starmoon S. Elgar

Alchemist-Jinade Leon D. Ellick
Pepsi Chantel Elliott
Atilla Albatros [*sic*] Emin
Bianca Marie England
Celestial Tranquillity-Te Ericsson-Zenith
Good Evans
Stephen Desire A. Fanny
Heather Feather
Scooter J. Foody
Princess Diana Frempong
Czar David Frost
Deborah Fuxall
Kraken James Gardiner
Tucker Capability Gibbs
Elizabeth Ecstacy Girling
Ocean Tsunami Golden
Laurel Olivia Hardy
Finn Vast Harrigan
Heidi Heidt
Porsche Carrera Hobday
Wendy House
William Incredible S. Hudghton
Phil Mike Hunt
Albert Einstein Huynh
Tanya Hyde
Rapunzel Hannah Inskip

Lyron Android Johnson

Indiana Jones

Quorum Scorpion B. Kevan

Brittany Merin Knickerbocker

Jedi Key-Ras-Tafari S. Knight

Lorraine Popoola Leak

Chandler Lear

Zsi Zsi A. Le Scrooge

Raphaella Bobcat J. Lewis

Alchemy Arcadia K. Lucas

Amanda Lynn

Merriment Marmite C. Mistrano

Sal Monella

Trudy Moody

Fay Mousley

Orapin Nonthing

Goodluck Brick Ogbogbo

Radar Oo

Drew Peacock

Casey Pancake Pickup

Tarzan Elvis Quennell

Dawn Raid

Lollipop Mae Richardson

Slayhne El Nasty Robinson

Vicky Ruff-Cock

Gonad Saghir

Frisbee C. C. Sheffield
Ray Sing
Cezanne Smith
Glorious Smith
Yawn H. H. Smith
Zenier Snowball Snowball
Dinah Soare
Coursamy Suckalingum
Lew Swires
Confetti Ngounou Tabe
Yumi Takeshita
Platinum Che'yrael Townsend
Jago Pirate Turner
Phoenix Claw Unicorn
Buster Beowulf Ratcliffe Van Der Geest
Valour Vespasian Vanglaive
Bee C. Wee
Auk Welch
Doctor Who
Ocean Storm Wise
Quasimodo W. T. Yeung
Harry Zona

FURTHER READING

Although the subject of unusual British names is mentioned in passing in numerous general books on names, this is the first book devoted to the subject. There is therefore no bibliography as such, but I would like to pay tribute to some nineteenth-century writers who observed the phenomenon of odd names, notably:

In an uncharacteristic display of humour for an official publication, the *Sixteenth Annual Report of the Registrar-General of Births, Deaths, and Marriages in England* (London: HMSO, 1856) included 'A list of peculiar surnames in England and Wales, selected from the Indexes of Births registered in the Quarter ending 31st March 1851, and of Deaths registered in the corresponding Quarter of 1853.'

Names that form themes (food, animals, musical instruments and so on) were identified and listed by the Lewes antiquarian Mark Antony Lower in his magisterial *Patronymica Britannica: A Dictionary of the Family Names of the United Kingdom* (Lewes: G. P. Bacon, 1860) and by Christopher Legge Lordan of Romsey in his *Of Certain English Surnames and their Occasional Odd Phases When Seen in Groups* (London: Houlston & Sons, 1874).

In 1892, Allen Batchelor, a Guildford hairdresser and umbrella-maker, published a poster featuring *An Alphabetical List of Over 2200 Curious Surnames of Her Majesty's Subjects*, 'especially adapted for education in all places where the working classes assemble, such as Coffee and Dining Rooms, Institutions, Inns, Public Houses, Solicitors' and other Offices, Political Clubs, and especially at Railway Stations'. (It's good to know that Victorian plebs could be educated as they waited for their trains.)

Charles Wareing Bardsley, *Curiosities of Puritan Nomenclature* (London: Chatto & Windus, 1897) is an exhaustive survey of all those Praise-god and Fly-fornication names.

◆

ACKNOWLEDGEMENTS

Warm thanks to my family, Caroline, Alexander and Nicholas Ash, Felicity and Julian Page, my agent John Saddler and my editors Val Hudson and Lorraine Jerram, who have all encouraged me in the project – despite my endlessly presenting them all with yet another strange name and asking, 'what do you think of this?' To their names, I should like to add those of Paul Dickson, Robert Easton, Cassie and Rory Fairhead, Virginia Nicholson, Barry Simner, Augusta Skidelsky and Howard Spencer.

Thanks are also due to Gerry Toop and the staff of the National Archives and Family Record Centre and the many county record offices and their dedicated archivists and researchers – especially those with senses of humour*. They include: Bedfordshire – James Collett-White; Cambridgeshire – Gill Shapland; Cheshire – Caroline Picco; Cumbria – David Bowcock; Devon – Renée Jackaman; Dorset – A. Munro; Gloucestershire – Pauline Nash; Herefordshire – John Harnden; Hertfordshire – Bonnie West; Isle of Wight – Richard Smout; Lancashire – John Benson; Lincolnshire – Mike Rogers; Norfolk – Claire Bolster; Northamptonshire – Eleanor Winyard; Nottinghamshire – William Bell; Pembrokeshire – Nikki Bosworth; Shropshire – Alison

Some failed to get the joke: I was assured that no one in the Isle of Man has ever had a silly name – so Arsey Cubbin, Rob Fuck and Easter Loony are clearly considered commonplace thereabouts

Healey; Somerset – Liz Grant; Suffolk – Dave Feakes; West
Sussex – Richard Childs.

The Cornwall Record Office deserves special mention for
its inspirational 'Silly Names List', compiled by archivist
Renée Jackaman (now at the Devon Record Office). Although
this has since been removed from the CRO website, I am
grateful to Renée for granting permission for it to appear on
mine—see: www.RussellAsh.com/CornwallSillyNames.

And finally, all the volunteers who have valiantly (and
sometimes imaginatively) transcribed often almost
indecipherable records.

THE END*

*Fanny End, died Reading, Berkshire, 1865